CLAUDE R. ALEXANDER JR.

BECOMING

THE

CHURCH

GOD'S PEOPLE IN
PURPOSE AND POWER

An imprint of InterVarsity Press
Downers Grove, Illinois

InterVarsity Press
P.O. Box 1400 | Downers Grove, IL 60515-1426
ivpress.com | email@ivpress.com

InterVarsity Press® is the publishing division of InterVarsity Christian Fellowship/USA®. For more information, visit intervarsity.org.

All Scripture quotations, unless otherwise indicated, are taken from The Holy Bible, New International Version®, NIV®. Copyright © 1973, 1978, 1984, 2011 by Biblica, Inc.™ Used by permission of Zondervan. All rights reserved worldwide. www.zondervan.com. The "NIV" and "New International Version" are trademarks registered in the United States Patent and Trademark Office by Biblica, Inc.™

While any stories in this book are true, some names and identifying information may have been changed to protect the privacy of individuals.

The publisher cannot verify the accuracy or functionality of website URLs used in this book beyond the date of publication.

Cover design and image composite: David Fassett
Interior design: Daniel van Loon

ISBN 978-1-5140-0572-9 (print) | ISBN 978-1-5140-0573-6 (digital)

Printed in the United States of America ∞

Library of Congress Cataloging-in-Publication Data
A catalog record for this book is available from the Library of Congress.

29 28 27 26 25 24 23 22 | 13 12 11 10 9 8 7 6 5 4 3 2 1

CONTENTS

INTRODUCTION

BEING AND BECOMING

I love the church of the Lord Jesus Christ. I realize that we live in an age where fewer are making that statement. However, I love the church.

I am painfully aware that those who don't love the church, who wish the church would disappear forever, feel that way in part due to an experience with some people who make up the church. To you, I offer my sincerest apologies. As those who are in the process of being made into the image of Christ, at times we miss the mark and fall tragically short, to God's dishonor, to our disappointment, and to a watching world's disdain. Yet God has not and does not give up on the church; neither do I. My hope is that in reading this, neither will you.

The church is God's idea. It is what Christ is building upon himself. It is that into which God calls every person who accepts his Son by faith.

I contend that the reason why many who've been added to the church don't move to being the church that God intends, is that they never understood what God intends for the church to be. You can't be or become what you don't understand.

This is not new. Those who made up the original members of the church didn't even get it all the time. In fact, the

Gospels, the book of Acts, and the New Testament Epistles are all God's way of helping them and us understand what God intends for the church to be and to do. The three years that they were with Jesus, and the time after his ascension into heaven, were all about becoming God's people in purpose and power.

As I write to you, I have been a part of the church for fifty of my fifty-seven years of life. I have learned that we who make up the church are both being *and* becoming. We both are the church and are still in the process of becoming the church. John, an apostle of Jesus, speaks to this: "Beloved, now we are children of God; and it has not yet been revealed what we shall be, but we know that when He is revealed, we shall be like Him, for we shall see Him as He is" (1 John 3:2 NKJV).

In the following pages, we will look at the disciples during the period immediately after Jesus' resurrection, through the Gospels as well as the first six chapters of the book of Acts. We will hear from some of them in their own voices and from their own perspectives in terms of their continual discovery and development into God's people in purpose and power.

Like the original members of the church, I am continuing to be led into becoming what God has in mind; a person of purpose and power. My hope is that I can better be who and what God has in mind. I invite you to do the same.

1

IF YOU GET JESUS,
YOU GET THE CHURCH

THOMAS

That Sunday evening the disciples were meeting behind locked doors because they were afraid of the Jewish leaders. Suddenly, Jesus was standing there among them! "Peace be with you," he said. As he spoke, he showed them the wounds in his hands and his side. They were filled with joy when they saw the Lord! Again he said, "Peace be with you. As the Father has sent me, so I am sending you." Then he breathed on them and said, "Receive the Holy Spirit. If you forgive anyone's sins, they are forgiven. If you do not forgive them, they are not forgiven."

One of the twelve disciples, Thomas (nicknamed the Twin), was not with the others when Jesus came. They told him, "We have seen the Lord!"

But he replied, "I won't believe it unless I see the nail wounds in his hands, put my fingers into them, and place my hand into the wound in his side."

Eight days later the disciples were together again, and this time Thomas was with them. The doors were locked; but suddenly, as before, Jesus was standing among them. "Peace be with you," he said. Then he said to Thomas, "Put your finger here, and look at my hands. Put your hand into the wound in my side. Don't be faithless any longer. Believe!"

"My Lord and my God!" Thomas exclaimed.

Then Jesus told him, "You believe because you have seen me. Blessed are those who believe without seeing me." (John 20:19-29 NLT)

Those who know my story would probably label me a contrarian. I am one whose life with Christ demonstrates doing the opposite of what most would do. For instance, many so-called believers would never miss Resurrection Sunday. In fact, if they don't go to church on any other Sunday, they go to church on Resurrection Sunday, yet the following Sunday they are nowhere to be seen or found. Churches boast record attendance on Resurrection Sunday.

If you know my story, you know that I am the exact opposite. I was nowhere near the church on the first Resurrection Sunday. While I was one of the initial members of Jesus' ministry and I was consistent in my followership and service for the first three years of the ministry's existence, on the first Resurrection Sunday I was not among the followers of Jesus. I was not found to be present in the fellowship of believers. On the most significant day of our existence as a body of Jesus-followers, I was not present.

In part, my absence was due to having experienced the most painful thing in my life just days earlier. On Thursday night, Jesus had been betrayed by one of our own, named Judas, falsely accused by dishonest witnesses, and mistried by the Sanhedrin Council. Early that Friday, he was examined by Pilate who found no wrong in him. But out of concern for the crowd and his political livelihood, Pilate sentenced Jesus to be crucified anyway. After Jesus had been brutally beaten, they crucified him. With each blow of the hammer to the nails in Jesus' hands and feet, my joy, hope, and faith were beaten to a pulp. It was the darkest period of my life, as I witnessed my hope painfully and publicly executed.

With Jesus being dead, I saw no reason to stay. Jesus was the reason I was in the group in the first place. I responded to Jesus' call to follow him. I was connected to the group due to their having received the same call. I didn't know the other eleven before Jesus. Jesus called us together. Our life together was due to our common acceptance of and life with Jesus. I wasn't there for them. I was there for Jesus.

Jesus was crucified. Jesus died. The only person who could raise anybody from the dead was dead himself. With

Jesus gone, there wasn't any reason for me to be there with them. I didn't get the church. I did not understand, then, that Jesus called us both to himself and to each other. He wasn't just calling us to be with him, but to be together with him and to be with him together.

JESUS' BODY

I had yet to grasp that my commitment to him was intertwined with my commitment to them, and that his development of me was and would continue to be within the context of connection to a body of believers. I didn't understand the fact that I couldn't fully get him if I did not get his people. *You can't get Jesus without also getting his body, the church.*

I didn't get the church. I could barely take some of them with Jesus around. Jesus was what made some of them bearable. Peter was hotheaded and temperamental. James and John were power hungry, wanting to have the best seats in the kingdom. Judas was a covetous thief who was siphoning off our money for himself. Nathanael was a cultural purist who didn't think that any good thing could come out of certain environments. Simon the Zealot was always talking about revolution. The only one who made sense to me and who made my time meaningful was Jesus. Now, Jesus was dead. With his death, with his departure, I left. Who stays in a place where the treasurer sells the leader out for a few pieces of silver? Who stays after one of the inner circle denies knowing his teacher, not once but three times? Who remains with a group that ran and left their Lord behind?

If I were being truly transparent, I couldn't put it all on the fact that I had suffered disappointment and disillusionment with Jesus' death and with Jesus' people, but I was also disappointed in myself. On that weekend, I really had a hard time looking at myself in the mirror. Everything that I could say about the others, they could say about me. I didn't live up to everything that I said I'd be or do

Leading up to the week that you all call Holy Week, there was the incident with Lazarus of Bethany. We got word that Lazarus was sick. Two days later, Jesus talked about going to raise Lazarus. We didn't have any problem with Jesus wanting to raise Lazarus from the dead, but we did have a problem with going to that area. The folks in Judea tried to stone Jesus the last time that we were there. We weren't feeling being stoned, but Jesus was persistent in going to raise Lazarus from the dead. Seeing that, I said, "Let us also go, that we may die with him" (John 11:16).

I was the one who said that I wasn't going to let Jesus face anything by himself. I was the one who said that I'd go and die with him. Yet, when the time came to stand with Jesus in death, I fled like everybody else. I let myself down, and I let Jesus down. I didn't want to face the eyes of those who might look at me knowing that I didn't do what I so boldly said that I would do.

So I left. I left the fellowship. I "de-churched." If you were to check the record, I was the first person to occupy the category of the de-churched. The de-churched are those who were once faithful to the assembled gathering of believers, who for one reason or another, exit the assembly.

I de-churched. Why continue in a group of messed up people? I could do bad all by myself. If by some miracle Jesus would rise from the dead, would he show up to the ones who let him down?

A PLACE OF GATHERING

So I left. Hurt by life, disillusioned with others, and disappointed with myself, I de-churched. On the first Resurrection Sunday, when Jesus actually got up from the dead and showed himself alive, I was not there. With me absent, Jesus showed up where the body gathered was. While I had a problem with them, Jesus showed up where they were. Jesus showed up where the body showed up. To the fearful and the failed, Jesus shows up. Jesus shows up in the midst of the church keeping its commitment.

Though far from perfect, they kept their commitment. I had forgotten his words, "For where two or three gather in my name, there am I with them" (Matthew 18:20). He didn't qualify the characteristics of the two or three. He did not call them perfect people. He did not say that they had to have it all together. It's not their perfection; it's his presence. It's their commitment to gathering together in his name. His presence makes up for their imperfection—their perfection is in him.

As faulty, flawed, and fearful as they were, they maintained their commitment to gather together in his name. Having gathered together in his name, Jesus kept his promise and made himself known in resurrection power and glory.

The wonder of the church is that it is the body through which God has chosen to make Jesus known and felt by the world. The fellowship of believers is the place where the promised presence of the Lord is most fully felt and found, where the people have the singular purpose of gathering together in the name of the Lord. Where there is a commitment to gather in his name, he is committed to making himself known, felt, and found. The distinction of the church is not in its facilities. It's not in its technology. It's not in its music. *Becoming the church involves appreciating that the distinction of the church is in the purpose of her gathering.* The church gathers together in the name of the Lord Jesus. The church gathers together for the purpose of the person and presence of the Lord Jesus Christ. It's the commitment to gather in his name. It's not about the perfection of character. It's about the sincerity and consistency of the commitment to gather together in his name.

COMMUNICATING OUR CONFESSION

It wasn't simply their commitment to gather together in his name, they were also communicating their confession.

Luke provides some information about what was happening: As they were talking about their experience with the resurrected Jesus, Jesus showed up. As they spoke about their experience with Jesus, Jesus showed up. As they were collectively talking about Jesus, Jesus showed up.

Becoming the church is recognizing the uniqueness of the content of our conversation—we have a confessional conversation. The church has a unique story to tell: We talk about the love of God in Christ Jesus displayed in the most graphic of terms. We talk about Jesus dying on a cross for the sins of the world. We talk about Jesus being buried in a grave. We dare to declare that Jesus was raised from the dead and is alive forevermore. We declare that he was seen by the women who went to the tomb; he was seen by the two on the road to Emmaus; he was seen by the Twelve; he was seen by more than five hundred followers before his ascension; he was seen by Paul on the road to Damascus; he was seen by John on the Isle of Patmos. We declare our having met him for ourselves. We declare what he's done in our lives.

In the midst of that conversation, the Lord makes himself known. He makes himself felt and found. There is a sense of him that is experienced whenever his people come together and talk about him. In the midst of their testimony, Jesus comes and confirms the truth of their confession. He is alive.

I was absent from the fellowship, and Jesus showed up and spoke peace to the people. He sought to calm their fears, still their agitation, and resolve their tension. I missed that move—I needed that peace. I needed that stillness. I needed that resolution.

The church is the place of proclaimed peace. It is in the midst of the body gathered that the Lord shows up to speak peace. Before Jesus died, he willed his peace to us as we gathered together in the upper room. He said, "Peace I leave with you; my peace I give you. I do not give to you as the world gives. Do not let your hearts be troubled and do not be afraid" (John 14:27). Having willed his peace to us prior to his death, Jesus showed up to the church gathered on Resurrection Sunday and again proclaimed peace to those who were gathered.

The church is the place of proclaimed peace. It is in the presence of the Lord's people that the presence of Christ is able to mediate a unique sense of peace that quiets, settles, assures, upholds, and sustains. There is something uniquely powerful when God's people are together and a word of peace is declared and collectively affirmed and received.

PEACE AND PURPOSE

Having shown himself alive to them, Jesus said to them, "As the Father has sent me, I am sending you" (John 20:21). Jesus spoke and clarified their purpose. They were apostles. They were to be sent persons. They were people with a mission. The mission was no less than the continuance of Jesus' mission. As the Father sent Jesus, so Jesus was sending us. The purpose of the group was assigned and clarified. But I was not present—I missed out on the assignment and clarification of my purpose in God. Our assignment was given within the context of our life together. *The church, being the place of expressed commitment, shared confession, and proclaimed peace, is also the place of assignment clarification.*

There are some levels of assignment and clarification that don't come in the isolation of your individuality. They come in the context of your existence within the body of Christ-followers. Jesus came to the upper room and let those who were there understand that their lives were to be lived missionally. They were on mission. They were on assignment. They were under orders. They were sent as Jesus had been sent. They were sent to continue the work of the kingdom of God. They were sent to continue the work of redemption.

I missed that experience. I needed to know what to do next. I needed to know the next steps of my life. I needed to know the rhyme and reason for the next things of God for me. I needed to know the flow and the stream wherein my life would now be lived.

The church is the place where God clarifies his assignment. In Acts 13, it's in the midst of the believers ministering to the Lord and fasting that the Holy Spirit assigns and clarifies Barnabas and Saul's purpose, saying, "Set apart for me Barnabas and Saul for the work to which I have called them" (Acts 13:2). It's in the midst of the saints that God can show up and reveal the next things of your life. It's in the midst of the Christ-followers that God can speak to you about the flow and stream wherein he has called you to walk. It's among the believers that God can remind you of the missional nature of your life. He puts you in remembrance that you are one who's been sent. He's saved you to live a sent life. You're under assignment and you're on a mission. There is no time in your life when you lack meaning and purpose. Every day of your life has meaning and purpose. Every day, there is an assignment. You are assigned to be the presence of the Lord wherever you are. You are assigned to be the incarnation of the love of God in the world.

There are times when life can throw you off track. There are times when things are not as clear as they once were. But it's in the midst of the body of believers that the Lord is able to show up and clarify. He shows up and lifts the darkness. He shows up and removes the scales. He shows up and dissipates the fog and the haze. He shows up with a word or a testimony that gives me an aha moment.

THE POWER OF THE SPIRIT

To the body of disciples that I left, Jesus showed up and revealed himself to be alive, spoke peace, clarified his assignment, and breathed power. Jesus breathed on those who were present and said, "Receive the Holy Spirit" (John 20:22). The word for *breathed* is one that is used one time in Genesis 2:7 where God breathed on Adam and he became a living soul. Here Jesus did the same thing to those who were in the room. He breathed upon them the Holy Spirit and told them to receive, take into themselves, and lay hold of the Spirit. He knew that they would need the guidance and the power of the Holy Spirit to live the lives to which they were called, so he gave them a breath of the Holy Spirit. Before leaving, he would tell all of us to wait in Jerusalem for the promise of the Father which was the Holy Spirit.

My friends, there is no way that you can live the lives of purpose to which you've been called in the natural. You can't do it on sheer intellect. You need spiritual power. You need the Lord to breathe on you. You need the Lord to give you power from on high. *Becoming the church entails the valuing of the church as the place where spiritual power is bestowed.* There's something about being in the midst of the body where the Lord has promised to be in the midst himself. There is a level of anointing that God provides within the collective body that you don't get individually. Every time that you gather together with other believers in the name of Jesus, you should come desiring and expecting the Lord to breathe upon you again. There should be a hunger and anticipation for the Lord to give you a fresh wind of the Spirit, which renews your strength in your inner person and gives you boldness to face an uncertain world one more time. You can't afford to live one week without the power of God. In truth, you can't live one day without God's power.

I didn't get all that the church was or what I was called to become. Because of that, I wasn't there when Jesus showed up. Afterward, hearing them talk about the experience, I said, "Unless I see the nail marks in his hands and put my finger where the nails were, and put my hand into his side, I will not believe" (John 20:25).

I needed to experience what they experienced. I needed to see what they saw. I needed to feel what they felt. I desired to have what they had. So, I went back to them.

The next day came, and I was there. I was there, and Jesus didn't show. The next day came, and I was there. Jesus didn't show. I wasn't going to be dissuaded. I made up in my mind that I was going to be there. I wasn't going to be absent when the Lord showed up again. In fact, it took eight days before he showed up again.

There are times when the body is gathered and there may not be the experience of the pervasively tangible presence of God. Don't be fooled into removing yourself from the midst. The moment that you move may be the moment that the Lord shows up.

CONFRONTING AND CONVICTING

On the eighth day, which would be the Sunday after Easter, Jesus showed up. This time, I was in the number. When he came, he spoke peace to us all. It was a peace that I needed to hear. I was wondering if I had missed my moment. I was wondering if my chance had passed me by. He spoke peace to everybody including me. Then, he came up to me and spoke to me. In the midst of my doubt, in the midst of what I didn't get about him and his people, he showed up and directed his attention toward me.

He said, "Put your finger here; see my hands. Reach out your hand and put it into my side. Stop doubting and believe" (John 20:27). This wasn't the time to address James or John. This was not the time to resolve Peter's issue. Jesus stepped up and spoke to my issue, my imperfection, and my sin. Everybody has an issue. Everybody has a hang-up. Everybody has something that Jesus could blast if he were so inclined. While others would have their days of confrontation, today was my day to be personally confronted by Jesus.

He came into the midst with me on his mind. He came with me on his agenda. He came to answer my questions. He came to build my faith. He came to change my perspective.

Becoming the church is comprehending that the church is the place where God uniquely confronts us and convicts us. The church is the place where God is able to focus uniquely on one in the midst of all of the others who are gathered.

With everyone else in the building, he will show up with you on the agenda. He will show up to answer your questions, to resolve your doubts, to calm your fears, to build your faith, to change your perspective.

Can you attest to the Lord having come in the midst and meeting you right where you are, coming as if you were the only one in the room? He sits down not just in your aisle, but in your seat. He gives you exactly what you need. In that moment, you can't help but be glad that you are in the number.

Jesus confronted me in my faithlessness, in my double-mindedness, in my skepticism and judgment of others. I was overwhelmed by the presence of the Lord. I was taken by the fact that the Lord would come with me in mind. I was totally taken by the glory of the Lord. The only thing that I could do was say, "My Lord and my God!" (John 20:28). Having been confronted, I was convicted. I came under the personal conviction of who Jesus is. He is my Lord and my God.

The only thing that I could do was praise the Lord. The only thing that I could do was offer the language of glory. The only thing that I could do was declare Jesus to be Lord and God. I'm so glad that I was there.

Jesus told me that I believed because I saw, but that blessed were those who would not see but yet believe. There are those of you in that category. You didn't get to put your fingers in his hands or your hands in his side, but you believe. You can talk about the church being the place where Jesus comes to confront you and to convict you. He confronts you with the truth of your sin. He convicts you of your sinfulness. He convinces you of the love of God demonstrated through his dying on the cross.

Having been confronted and convicted, you can declare your belief. You believe that Jesus died for you. You believe that God raised Jesus for you. You know the blessing of believing. You know the joy of believing. You know the peace of believing. You know what it is to have your sins forgiven and to have your life made brand new. You can testify about the blessing of believing in him. You've declared "My Lord and My God." Having gotten Jesus, you also get his church.

2

SECOND CHANCES

PETER

Afterward Jesus appeared again to his disciples, by the Sea of Galilee. It happened this way: Simon Peter, Thomas (also known as Didymus), Nathanael from Cana in Galilee, the sons of Zebedee, and two other disciples were together. "I'm going out to fish," Simon Peter told them, and they said, "We'll go with you." So they went out and got into the boat, but that night they caught nothing.

Early in the morning, Jesus stood on the shore, but the disciples did not realize that it was Jesus.

He called out to them, "Friends, haven't you any fish?"

"No," they answered.

He said, "Throw your net on the right side of the boat and you will find some." When they did, they were unable to haul the net in because of the large number of fish.

Then the disciple whom Jesus loved said to Peter, "It is the Lord!" As soon as Simon Peter heard him say, "It is the Lord," he wrapped his outer garment around him (for he had taken it off) and jumped into the water. The other disciples followed in the boat, towing the net full of fish, for they were not far from shore, about a hundred yards. When they landed, they saw a fire of burning coals there with fish on it, and some bread.

Jesus said to them, "Bring some of the fish you have just caught." So Simon Peter climbed back into the boat and dragged the net ashore. It was full of large fish, 153, but even with so many the net was not torn. Jesus said to them, "Come and have breakfast." None of the disciples dared ask him, "Who are you?" They knew it was the Lord. Jesus came, took the bread and gave it to them, and did the same with the fish. This was now the third time Jesus appeared to his disciples after he was raised from the dead.

When they had finished eating, Jesus said to Simon Peter, "Simon son of John, do you love me more than these?"

"Yes, Lord," he said, "you know that I love you."

Jesus said, "Feed my lambs."

Again Jesus said, "Simon son of John, do you love me?"

He answered, "Yes, Lord, you know that I love you."

Jesus said, "Take care of my sheep."

> The third time he said to him, "Simon son of John, do
> you love me?"
>
> Peter was hurt because Jesus asked him the third time,
> "Do you love me?" He said, "Lord, you know all things;
> you know that I love you."
>
> Jesus said, "Feed my sheep. Very truly I tell you, when
> you were younger you dressed yourself and went
> where you wanted; but when you are old you will
> stretch out your hands, and someone else will dress you
> and lead you where you do not want to go." Jesus said
> this to indicate the kind of death by which Peter would
> glorify God. Then he said to him, "Follow me!"
> (John 21:1-19)

You just read about Thomas and his need to get the church. He talked about his failure to realize that you can't get Jesus without getting his body, which is the church. Thomas shared the need to appreciate the purpose of the church's gathering, the uniqueness of the content of its conversation. He also shared about the church as being the place of proclaimed peace, of assignment clarification, of the bestowal of spiritual power, and of personal confrontation and conviction.

It would be wonderful if the story of our early beginning was limited to Thomas's absence and return. However, Thomas wasn't the only one to de-church. I was the second to de-church. It was some time after the experience on the eighth day when Jesus came and specifically engaged Thomas. To be sure, it was quite an experience when Jesus showed up and challenged Thomas to put his finger where the print of his hand was and to put his hand where the hole in his side was. Everybody was amazed at how Jesus repeated verbatim what Thomas had said to us in Jesus' physical absence; his charge for Thomas to stop doubting and to believe was powerful. So powerful that Thomas exclaimed what many of us felt, "My Lord and my God!" I was happy for Thomas. He received what he needed.

However, I was still at a point of unrest and unease. To be sure, I was elated that Jesus was alive. But I also was troubled. The message that he gave the women at the tomb was to tell the disciples and me—Peter—that he was risen and that he'd meet us in Galilee. He mentioned me by name; he singled me out.

I really didn't know what to make of that then. In his first several appearances there was nothing directed specifically at me to give me further clarity.

I deeply regretted my threefold denial of Jesus. At my third denial, when the rooster crowed, Jesus turned and looked straight at me from across the courtyard. I'll never forget the look on his face and the pathos in his eyes. I broke down and wept bitterly. I failed the Lord—I didn't keep my word to him. So I left.

I returned to the fellowship that night. I was there Saturday and Sunday. Then John and I went to the tomb and saw that it was empty, we saw the grave clothes folded. We saw Jesus later that evening. He appeared eight days later, but still no word to me. No mention about what happened.

I started to wonder what was on Jesus' mind concerning me. What was Jesus thinking and feeling about me? I know how badly I felt about myself. Is that how he felt about me? I know that there were moments I couldn't look at myself in the mirror. Was it hard for him to look at me? Is that why he hadn't said anything?

I not only wondered what was on Jesus' mind, I also wondered what kind of life I would have when he departed. He'd been talking about going back to the Father. What did that mean for me? What could I count on when he left? I knew what my life was like before I met Jesus. I knew the routine that I had. I knew the level of comfort and challenge that I had. I also knew what life was like for three years with Jesus. I knew the highs and the lows. I knew the ups and the downs. I knew the demands, the risks, the costs, and indeed the sacrifice.

One day, when I was with Thomas, Nathanael, James, John, and two of the others, I decided to go out to fish. By fishing, I didn't mean the fishing to which Jesus had called me. That was for people. I mean the fishing that I was doing before Jesus showed up. The last time that I was found fishing was prior to Jesus calling me to follow him. In fact, when he called me and my brother Andrew, we immediately left our nets and followed him.

But now, I was going out to fish. I de-churched. There was something easier. There was something less stressful. There was something less weighty. I was going out to fish. Fishing for fish was not as much trouble as fishing for people. It was easier to catch and to clean fish. Catching people who don't want to be caught and discipling people who don't want to be discipled was a hassle. I was going out to fish. I was good at fishing for fish. I knew what it meant to fish for fish. I could halfway control fishing for fish.

LIVING IN THE TENSION

I was between points of revelation. I had received the resurrection revelation, but I had yet to receive the restoration revelation. I had yet to know what that meant for my life. I had yet to get the "so what" revelation.

Perhaps you know what it is to exist between points of revelation. You have one piece of the puzzle, but there is another piece that is outstanding. There is the temptation to try to fill in the blanks by resorting to what is familiar. In the midst of the ambiguous, there is the penchant for returning to the tried-and-true. When you are between points of revelation, you find yourself in the tension between waiting on the next word and going on your own based on the comfort of the past.

Standing in the gap between points of revelation and following Jesus into an uncertain future is risky business. For some it is so much easier to fill in the blank with what we know. It's easier to return to the substandard relationship than to be alone with Jesus. It's easier to blend in with everyone else in mediocrity than to stand out in excellence. It's easier to reduce the goal to where we've already been, what we've already done, and what we've already given, than to stand in the gap and hear Jesus call us to step out of the box and do what hasn't been done, go where we haven't been, and to give at a level that we've never given.

So I said, "I'm going out to fish"; I'm out. The others said, "We'll go with you." Seven of the eleven of us were out. We were back to what we knew before Jesus interrupted our schedule and overturned our agenda. We were back to the comfortable and the predictable.

We didn't get the fact that *the church lives within the tension of existing between points of revelation.* There is always a missing piece. We are never given the full picture. There are times that we are told the what or the that, but when is left out. There are times when where is left out. There are times when who is left out. There are times when how is left out. We live between points of revelation. We dwell in the already but not yet.

As such, we must resist the tendency to fill in the blanks ourselves and resort to who we were, where we were, and how we were. It's better to stand between points of revelation than return to periods of irrelevance.

FRIENDSHIP AND FRUITFULNESS

There we were out on the sea. We fished all night and caught nothing. This was oddly familiar. We experienced the same results that we had before we met Jesus. We fished all night long and caught nothing. Jesus asked us, "Friends, haven't you any fish?" (John 21:5). This question struck us on two levels. The first level was with the word *friends*. The last time that he used that word was when he told us, "Greater love has no one than this: to lay down one's life for one's friends. You are my friends if you do what I command" (John 15:13-14). With that word *friends*, Jesus was raising the question whether or not our current action was in alignment with him. That word was an examining word: Were we out there on the sea by his command, as the result of his direction?

Might I pause and ask you how is your friend status with Jesus? Is your level of obedience such that Jesus would call you friend? Is the level of your alignment to his will such that Jesus would "friend" you? Is your level of surrender and submission to his command such that he would consider de-friending you?

If that word *friends* was not enough, the second level really hit us. He asked, had we caught anything? Were things any different now than they were before we met him? With us operating in pre-Jesus mode, were we getting post-Jesus results? The subtle trick of the enemy is to get you to think that you can return to a pre-Jesus mode and experience post-Jesus results. Whenever we fall into that trick, Jesus will show up and ask us, *Friend, have you caught anything? How is this working for you? Is it what you thought it would be? Is it all that it promised you? Does it compare to the life that you had when you were following me?*

We had to admit that we hadn't caught anything. We had nothing to show. We expended energy and were left with nothing.

We didn't get that *as the church, our fruitfulness is tied to simply abiding in him.* The fruitfulness of the church is in its remaining in Jesus. The primary call that he made to us was to be with him. We were called to him. Having been called to him, we were challenged to remain in him. He did tell us in John 15:5, "I am the vine; you are the branches. If you remain in me and I in you, you will bear much fruit; apart from me you can do nothing." It is as we live in him, allow ourselves to be shaped, directed, fed, and led by him, that his abundant power is able to flow to and through us, causing us to be fruitful.

FOLLOWING DIRECTION

Jesus made the point by telling us to cast our nets on the right side of the ship to find some fish. Again, at his direction, we cast our nets. Before, we cast our nets at our own direction. This time, we were challenged to cast our nets at his direction. He sought to reinforce that our calling was to live by his direction.

We needed to get the fact that *the church is one whose effectiveness is in following his direction.* "There is a way that appears to be right, but in the end it leads to death" (Proverbs 14:12). The end is futile. The end is empty. The end is vain.

A life in Christ calls us to know that our times are in his hands. He knows the way that we should take. His directions are based on knowing what's best and having what's best.

Maybe you can bear witness to trying to do it your own way before and failing every time, and you have experienced what the Lord produces when you do it his way. Now you've made up in your mind that you're going to trust in the Lord with all your heart and lean not unto your own understanding. In all your ways, you'll acknowledge him and let him direct your paths (Proverbs 3:5-6).

We cast our nets over to the right side expecting a catch. Within his direction there was a promise. The promise was that we would catch some. If we followed him, we wouldn't be disappointed.

There was promise in his direction. The promise within his direction gave fuel to our expectations. The fuel of our expectations gave strength to our obedience. We boldly threw our nets because we had a strong expectation due to his promise.

When you grasp the promise that's from the direction of the Lord, the expectation of that promise will overcome your fatigue and your disappointment. Our expectations overcame the fatigue of a night spent fishing. They overcame the disappointment of spending a night fishing and catching nothing. They overcame the conventional wisdom that the morning was not the best time to catch fish. They overcame the tapes that played, "We tried this before . . ."

OBEDIENCE AND GREATNESS

Jesus told us to cast our nets on the right side of the boat and we would find some fish. We didn't just find *some* fish, we found so many that we weren't able to haul in the net. The net was full of large fish, 153 in all. That's just like Jesus to do much more than what we thought. We discovered more than we imagined.

The word for *large* also means great, surprising, and significant. Jesus had something great and significant. While I sought to resort to a life of relative safety, Jesus was calling me to a life of significant greatness.

The church is the body that is called to catch the significant and the great through obedience. In our pursuit of Christ, in our obedience to him, Christ seeks to produce the significant and the great. The person who searches for significance and greatness in and of itself will often catch nothing. The person who seeks to obey Christ discovers that which is significant and great. In our obedience, we catch what is great, we connect with what is significant.

John immediately recognized Jesus. And then I jumped into the water to get to Jesus. I went from avoidance to engagement—I wanted to see Jesus. I didn't realize that Jesus wanted to see me more than I wanted to see him. My desire overcame my shame, my worry, my doubts. Jesus' presence made up for the gap between the points of revelation. I discovered that more than anything, I needed Jesus. More than another word, more than another work, I need Jesus.

LIVING WITH LOVE

When I got to where he was, I saw that he already had what I was trying to get. While I was fishing all night, catching nothing, Jesus already had some fish. Before he told us to cast our nets, he already had some fish.

I discovered that Jesus already has what we're trying to get. The peace that we're trying to get, Jesus already has. The joy that we're trying to get, Jesus already has. The love that we're trying to get, Jesus already has.

When we finished eating, Jesus asked me, "Simon son of John, do you truly love me more than these?"

I said, "Yes Lord, you know that I love you."

He said, "Feed my lambs." And again he asked me, "Simon son of John, do you love me?"

I answered, "Yes Lord, You know that I love you."

He said, "Take care of my sheep." Then a third time he said, "Simon son of John, do you love me?"

I said, "Lord you know all things; You know that I love you" (John 21:15-17).

After my threefold denial of him, Jesus was raising a threefold question centering around my loving him. He was reminding me that my denial was not a matter of knowledge or belief, it was a matter of love and devotion. My lack of courage was due to a faulty love and a weak devotion. In so doing, Jesus was seeking to reorient me from a life where I was at the center to a life where he was at the center. His purposes for me can't be fulfilled when he is at the periphery. He must be at the center. I must have a love for him that is primary.

The church is the community called to live with a love for Christ at the center. The fulfillment of our purpose comes not out of knowledge or even belief—it is out of a love for Jesus. This love is not an emotive love, it is a volitional love. It is not based on how we feel, it's based on who we choose to be and what we choose to do out of a commitment to the object of the love. The love of Christ will move us to publicly identify with him. We can't love him and not go public with him. We can't love him and keep him inside the house. Our love for him will motivate us to talk about him. Our love for him will cause us to take him with us outside the house. Our love for him will move us to let people know who he is, how he is, and what he's done. He is the center of our joy.

SACRIFICIAL SERVICE

I told him that I loved him. He then told me, "Feed my lambs. . . . Take care of my sheep. . . . Feed my sheep." He called me to serve in such a way that I see those whom I serve as belonging to him. He called me to a life outside of myself and into the lives of others. He redirected me from an inward and self focus, to an outward and others focus.

The church is the community of believers who are called to sacrificial service. The call of Christ is the call to come outside of ourselves into the lives of others. It is to move from a self-focus to an other-focus. It is the call to sacrificial service because it is the call to serve sheep and lambs. One characteristic about them is that they are primarily self-centered; sheep don't think about us, in fact sometimes, they don't think at all. If we are going to feed them and take care of them, we must sacrifice. We must exercise patience. We must come out of ourselves for their sake.

We do so because they are his. It is the love for Christ that prompts the desire to serve those who belong to Christ. The challenge to everyone in the service of Christ is to see those to whom we are called to serve as belonging to Christ. It is to see the children that we teach as belonging to Christ. It is to see the people that we counsel as belonging to Christ. It is to see the people that we protect as belonging to Christ. It is to see the people that we treat, that we represent, on whom we wait as belonging to Christ.

They are those for whom he died, for whom he was raised from the dead, and for whom he currently prays.

It is to serve by seeing them as the Lord sees us. In my rough and raw state, Jesus sees me as his. In my impetuous and impatient state, he sees me as his. In my foolish and flaky state, he sees me as his. The same is true for you. He sees you as his beloved, as the apple of his eye. He sees you being worth his effort. He sees you being worth his sacrifice. He sees you worth his sweat and worth his tears. He sees you worth his agony in the garden and worth his scourging in Pilate's courtyard. He sees you being worth the nails, worth the spear, worth the weight of sin, worth the darkness between the sixth and ninth hour, worth the last breath, worth the burial, worth descending into hell, and worth the resurrection. He sees us worth a second chance, a second look.

3

CALLED TO MISSION

MATTHEW

> Then the eleven disciples went to Galilee, to the mountain where Jesus had told them to go. When they saw him, they worshiped him; but some doubted. Then Jesus came to them and said, "All authority in heaven and on earth has been given to me. Therefore go and make disciples of all nations, baptizing them in the name of the Father and of the Son and of the Holy Spirit, and teaching them to obey everything I have commanded you. And surely I am with you always, to the very end of the age." (Matthew 28:16-20)

Some three years ago, my life was turned inside out and upside down. Maybe I should say right-side up. One day, while I was sitting at my tax collector's booth, extorting money from my own people, Jesus came to me and called me to follow him. Right where I was in the midst of moral and ethical wrongdoing, Jesus intersected and intervened. I can't explain the power of his presence and invitation. I left my booth with money still on the table. So taken was I with Jesus, that I threw a dinner party and invited all of my crew to meet Jesus.

He was the best thing that ever happened to me. I joined eleven others whom he had called to participate in a three-year intensive program with the kingdom of God as its subject matter. It was an experience unlike any other. There was nobody quite like Jesus. I could see spending my whole life traveling with him, listening to him, watching him work, and assisting him whenever he needed assistance. In fact, that's what I thought I had signed up for. As time passed, Jesus began to talk about being crucified and being raised from the dead. Toward the latter part of the third year, he added that he was going to go away and that where he was going, we would be there also.

I didn't get the point early on that the intensive three years were designed to prepare us to operate without his physical presence. It never occurred to me when we started with Jesus that within three years he would be gone and that we would be called to become his presence on the earth. I didn't get that he was making us to become his church.

However, with his death and resurrection, I began to get what he was doing and what he wanted us to be. The time that he spent with us post-resurrection and pre-ascension was invaluable. It laid the foundation for us to get what the church is and what we as the church should be about.

AN APPOINTMENT WITH JESUS

I share one of those occasions with you. Subsequent to his resurrection, Jesus told us to go to Galilee where we would see him. We had a scheduled appointment. We made our way to the mountain where he had told us to go. As we traveled, we saw him—Jesus kept his appointment. Jesus keeps his appointments! Jesus will be wherever he says that he will be. He will be there as he needs to be. He will be there when he needs to be.

He may not come when we think that he should, but he keeps his appointments on his time which is always on time. Jairus will testify that Jesus kept the appointment with him and his daughter. Mary and Martha will testify that Jesus kept his appointment with them and Lazarus. I can bear witness that he told us that he would be crucified on one day and be raised on the third day. He kept that appointment.

Jesus kept his appointment and we saw him. We recognized who he was. We knew that it was Jesus. We didn't just see Jesus the teacher, Jesus the healer, or Jesus the miracle worker. We saw Jesus the Lord. We were touched by his deity. Before us was the resurrected Son of God. For that reason, we worshiped him. At his birth, Magi bowed before him in worship. Now, upon his resurrection from the dead, we worshiped him. We lay prostrate before him.

I wish that I could tell you that everyone worshiped, that everyone bowed before him and gave their all to him, but I must present an honest and accurate account. Some doubted. Some were of a double mind. They were hesitant and uncertain. They didn't know what to make of what they were seeing. Was what they were seeing true? As a result, they held themselves back.

Such is the case for those given to doubt. They are of two minds. They are unable to give themselves to either thought. There are those who may readily acknowledge that Jesus died for the sins of the world, but they doubt that he died for them. Or they may believe that he died for their sins and accept him as Savior, but when it comes to his lordship and the implications for their lives, there is extreme hesitancy.

In the midst of the mixed atmosphere of worship and doubt, Jesus came to us. The closer that he came to us, the closer that he brought us to himself. Jesus is forever coming to us. The closer that he comes to us, the closer that he brings us to himself.

UNDER AUTHORITY

He not only came to us, but also he spoke to us. He wanted to assure us. He wanted our faith to be full. He spoke to resolve doubts, to confirm faith, and to infuse comfort. Every now and then, you need to hear a word from the Lord. When times and circumstances would cause you to be doubtful, hesitant, anxious, or uncertain, you need a word from the Lord to increase your faith, excite your hope, enliven your joy, and enhance your being. The good news is that he will speak to you. Often, he will start with something about himself—he will declare his lordship. "All authority in heaven and on earth has been given to me" (Matthew 28:18).

All power, the freedom of action, the power of rule, the ability and right to appoint, the right to require obedience, has been given. It was not usurped, it was not taken. It was given on the basis of his incarnation, death, burial, and resurrection. Because he took on himself the form of a servant and became obedient to death on the cross, God exalted him and gave him a name above every other name. At the name of Jesus, every knee will bow, in heaven, on earth, and under the earth, and every tongue will confess that Jesus is Lord, to the glory of God the Father (Philippians 2:7-11). "For this very reason, Christ died and returned to life so that he might be the Lord of both the dead and the living" (Romans 14:9).

Jesus' dominion is universal. He spoke of having power on earth to forgive sins; he now claims all power universally. In heaven he has power, for he reigns over the angels: "Angels, authorities and powers [are] in submission to him" (1 Peter 3:22). He has the vested authority of intercession with the Father. In earth, he has power; by him, kings reign and all souls are his.

Jesus' authority is why he could resist and reject the tempter who sought to get him to compromise. What the tempter was offering was less than what Jesus would receive through obedience. The tempter offered Jesus the unredeemed kingdoms of this world through compromise—God had more in mind for Jesus to receive through obedience. God had the authority of the redeemed earth and heaven in mind.

God always has more in mind through obedience than the tempter has in mind through compromise. Though what the tempter offers through compromise may seem easier, it neither lasts as long nor has what God desires for you through obedience. What the tempter offers may look good, but what God has is good, and perfect. The tempter may offer you something quick and easy, but it won't last and will hurt you more.

When Jesus met us in Galilee, he told us that all power had been given to him in heaven and in earth, assuring us that there is no locality where his authority and influence are not present. But he was telling us something more. Because he has the right to govern, and to require obedience in heaven and earth, he has the right to require obedience from us. He was alerting us that he had a claim on our lives.

The church is the body of believers who operate under his primary claim. Having died for us, having bought us with his blood, Christ is the primary lien holder on us. As Lord of heaven and earth, Christ is the primary authority. Every other claim is second to him and is subject to him. In fact, all others must be seen through and in terms of his claim. That's why when Peter and John stood before the Sanhedrin and were ordered to no longer preach or teach in the name of Jesus, they responded, "Which is right in

God's eyes: to listen to you, or to him? You be the judges! As for us, we cannot help speaking about what we have seen and heard" (Acts 4:19-20). Christ has the primary claim and is the primary authority. Jesus told us, when he sent us out two-by-two, "What I tell you in the dark, speak in the daylight; what is whispered in your ear, proclaim from the roofs. Do not be afraid of those who kill the body but cannot kill the soul. Rather, be afraid of the One who can destroy both soul and body in hell" (Matthew 10:27-28).

CALLED TO ACTION

The church operates under the authority of Christ who issues imperative statements. As the Lord of the church, the statements that Christ makes are not suggestive in nature. They are imperative in nature. They are not food for thought, they are commands for action. Because he has all authority in heaven and earth, he tells us, "Therefore go and make disciples of all nations" (Matthew 28:19). *The church is the community called to evangelistic movement.* Jesus commanded us to go, to make our way. He presses us into service, into action, beyond ourselves. With his authority being throughout the earth, Jesus sends us into all of the world. No longer the limited commission where we were banned from Gentile territory, now it is a worldwide commission. We are to go and carry the word into the world with the objective of making disciples for Jesus. We are to go with the aim of leading people into the realm and rule of Jesus.

The church is the body of believers who are charged with the task of evangelistic going. Jesus essentially says "*as* you go." Our lives are never simply to be about going here or there, they are to be about going with his purpose in mind. Wherever you go, you should have in mind pointing people to him. You should have in mind bringing people to a saving and growing relationship with him. In the midst of you going home, going to school, going to work, going to meetings, going shopping, going to the gym, going to lunch, going to dinner, going to the game, going to the movies, going to visit, going on vacation, the Lord says "Go and make disciples." Go for him and with him in mind.

FELLOWSHIP OF THE CONNECTED

We were not just called to evangelistic going. *The church is also the fellowship of the incorporated and the connected.* He told us to baptize them in the name of the Father, the Son, and the Holy Spirit. The first act of discipleship and obedience is the act of baptism. While baptism is not essential to salvation, it is essential to discipleship and obedience. We baptize because Christ commanded baptism. As an act of obedience, it demonstrates the beginning of God's reign in our lives and the process of conversion from a self-led life to a God-led life. It says that I'm not my own, I belong to him.

He gave us a formula that speaks of the movement from one point to another. He said, "In the name of the Father, the Son, and the Holy Spirit." The word *in* literally means "into." "Into the name" means the movement into the possession and relationship of the person named. It speaks to an oath of allegiance to and existing under the possession of the person named. Through baptism, we declare that we are in a relationship of being possessed, governed, owned, and having communion with the Father, Son, and Holy Spirit.

We have a relationship with the Father who created the world, who provides for every living thing, who preserves our souls, who loved us such that he sent his Son into the world, who holds us in his hands, and who secures us knowing that no one can pluck us out of his hands.

We identify with the Son, sent to be the propitiation of our sins, who loves us, who intercedes for us. We identify with his death, with his burial, and with his resurrection. We live in the hope of his return.

We are in relationship with the Holy Spirit, who revealed Jesus to us, who gave us the faith to call him Lord, who baptized us into the body, who filled us, who sealed us unto the day of redemption, who gifts us with spiritual gifts, who leads us into truth, who convicts us of sin, and who comforts us.

Through baptism, we become a part of the family of God. We are connected into a fellowship where there is mutual accountability. We are accountable to and accountable for one another. We are not alone. We are connected.

A LIFE OF DISCIPLINE

Jesus also told us "to teach them to obey everything that I commanded them." He wanted us to know that *the church is the community of the knowledgeable and disciplined.* The making of a disciple does not end with evangelism and baptism. It's not over with the right hand of fellowship, the receiving of a certificate, and the taking of a picture. There must be a continuation of teaching of what Jesus commanded. Jesus told us earlier, "If you continue in my word, you are truly my disciples; and you will know the truth, and the truth will make you free" (John 8:31-32 NRSV). He charged us with teaching. This is instruction for the building up of the body. It is moral teaching, it is the teaching of the kingdom life, it is teaching in righteousness—how to live uprightly within a fallen world. He commanded us to teach what it means to "Seek first his kingdom and his righteousness" (Matthew 6:33). We are commanded to teach how to live a life of love and service both to God and to humanity. People need to know how to cope with the changes and uncertainties of life. People need to know how to overcome evil with good. People must be given the way that is not of this world. The world teaches its way, a way of emptiness and destruction. *The church is the body with the way of Jesus that leads to life.*

This is not knowledge just for the sake of knowledge; it is teaching them to obey whatever he has commanded. This isn't about us getting our word to feel; this is about getting his word to obey. It's a life of discipline. It's about the word shaping and influencing our life, the choices that we make, the perceptions that we have, the responses that we give. It's about the word of Christ serving as the mediator of our thoughts and actions such that we hold fast to what he has commanded. It's holding fast to his teaching: "Let your light shine before others, that they may see your good deeds and glorify your Father in heaven" (Matthew 5:16); "Ask and it will be given to you; seek and you will find; knock and the door will be opened to you" (Matthew 7:7); and "Love your enemies, bless those who curse you, do good to those who hate you, and pray for those who spitefully use you and persecute you, that you may be sons of your Father in heaven" (Matthew 5:44-45 NKJV).

ETERNAL ASSURANCE

As I listened to Jesus, I thought: *This is a tall order that he's giving us.* He knew that it was a lot for us to take in. He knew that he couldn't end with just evangelistic movement, incorporation and connection, and knowledge and discipline. That's why he said, "And surely I am with you always, to the very end of the age." He knew that we needed some assurance, some promise, something to anchor us. *The church is the body of the eternally assured.* He wanted us to know that we wouldn't be alone. He said "with you." In the midst, in accompaniment, in participation, in association, in identity, in readiness, Jesus looked at us just like he and the Father looked at Moses. Moses, intimidated by the sign of his assignment, was assured by God with the words, "I will be with you" (Exodus 3:12). Looking at Joshua and the assignment given to him, God assured him with the words, "As I was with Moses, so I will be with you" (Joshua 1:5). Looking at Jeremiah and the assignment given to him, God said, "Do not be afraid of them, for I am with you and will rescue you" (Jeremiah 1:8).

Jesus was saying to us, "Surely, truthfully, certainly, definitely, absolutely, undoubtedly, surely, I am with you." As God sent Moses by the name *I Am*, so now Christ was speaking to us by the name. The same words that he had told us earlier, "Before Abraham was, I Am." I Am the Bread of Life, the Light of the World, the Door, the Good Shepherd, the Resurrection and the Life, the Way, the Truth, and the Life, the True Vine.

With us, he is. The One to whom past, present, and future are the same. With us he is whatever we would need for him to be—a shelter, a rock, a defender, a guide, a company keeper, a burden bearer, a heavy load sharer.

He will be with us always in the days of confidence, in the days of doubt, in the fair days, in the foul days, in the bright days, in the gloomy days, in the light days, in the dark days, in the warm days, in the cold days, in the high times, in the low times, in the full times, in the empty times, in the strong times, in the weak times, in the flourishing times, in the famished times.

In every way and in every place, when you walk through the fire, when you walk through the floods, on the mountain high and in the valley low, he'll be there. He won't change. He'll be there even to the end. Whenever the end is, he'll be there. The end is in him. He is from everlasting to everlasting.

Amen. So be it.

That is our assurance. To that we say "Amen."

4

PEOPLE OF PURPOSE

LUKE

In my former book, Theophilus, I wrote about all that Jesus began to do and to teach until the day he was taken up to heaven, after giving instructions through the Holy Spirit to the apostles he had chosen. After his suffering, he presented himself to them and gave many convincing proofs that he was alive. He appeared to them over a period of forty days and spoke about the kingdom of God. On one occasion, while he was eating with them, he gave them this command: "Do not leave Jerusalem, but wait for the gift my Father promised, which you have heard me speak about. For John baptized with water, but in a few days you will be baptized with the Holy Spirit." (Acts 1:1-5)

Thus far, you have read about Thomas, Peter, and Matthew. They were three individuals who began a journey with Jesus not knowing what Jesus intended for them. It wasn't until the middle of their three years with Jesus that they began to get what he was doing and what he wanted them to become. In fact, it wasn't until after Jesus' death and resurrection that they began to grasp this notion of their calling to become the church.

I found this particularly to be the case as I, Luke, set out to write the Gospel that bears my name as well as the book you know as Acts. Under the direction of the Holy Spirit, I was led to write a history of the church from its beginning, about the life of our Lord and his life with the Twelve. My goal was that my benefactor, Theophilus, would be certain of what he had been taught about Jesus. I would also write about the continuation of Jesus' work through the apostles and the church that God developed through them.

AN UNLIKELY PEOPLE

The latter part of Luke 24 serves as a bridge connecting that Gospel I wrote to the book of Acts. The setting is one of Jesus' face-to-face meetings with the remaining eleven disciples. Right here is a major point for you to know about the church: *The church is made up of unlikely people.*

In chapter 6 of my Gospel I share that, after a night of prayer, Jesus selected twelve from among those who were following him to be designated as apostles. They were Simon whom he named Peter, Andrew, James, John, Philip, Bartholomew, Matthew, Thomas, James son of Alphaeus, Simon called the Zealot, Judas son of James, and Judas Iscariot. None of them had any religious pedigree. Almost all of them, being Galilean, were held suspect by the Judeans as being irreligious. They weren't your regular temple or synagogue attendees. One of them, Matthew, was a confirmed public sinner and traitor of the nation as a tax collector. Judas Iscariot was skimming money from the top of the treasury. They were an unlikely crowd from the very beginning. There wasn't much to see from their three years with Jesus that gave a clue that they would be trusted with the church on his departure. They were given to inside squabbling about who would be the greatest; they were constantly missing the essence of what he was trying to say. Every now and then, there might be a flash of kingdom usefulness. But, they weren't making a lot of hay. When Jesus was arrested, they fled the scene. Judas betrayed Jesus. Peter denied him three times. The rest literally were out of sight.

It is to them, however, that Jesus appears after the resurrection. It is to them that he continually shows himself because they would be the ones into whose hands and upon whose lives the church spread. As unlikely as they were, they were the ones whom the Lord chose to use. As flawed, as imperfect, as blundering, as bungling as they were, they were the ones whom the Lord chose.

The church is made up of unlikely people. The apostle Paul reflects on this in 1 Corinthians 1:26-31:

Take a good look, friends, at who you were when you got called into this life. I don't see many of "the brightest and the best" among you, not many influential, not many from high-society families. Isn't it obvious that God deliberately chose men and women that the culture overlooks and exploits and abuses, chose these "nobodies" to expose the hollow pretensions of the "somebodies"? That makes it quite clear that none of you can get by with blowing your own horn before God. Everything that we have—right thinking and right living, a clean slate and a fresh start—comes from God by way of Jesus Christ. That's why we have the saying, "If you're going to blow a horn, blow a trumpet for God." (*The Message*)

None of us has anything that qualifies us to be trusted with the eternal riches of glory. All of us are unlikely.

He kept coming to them. He kept showing up to them. He kept teaching them because as unlikely and as unworthy as they may have been, they were chosen and called.

AN UNUSUAL PLACE

Not only is the church made up of unlikely people, but also *the church begins in and is constantly assigned to an unusual place*. Jesus told them not to leave Jerusalem, but to wait for the promise of the Father. Jerusalem was an unusual place to stay because it was not their home. Home for them was in cities such as Bethsaida, Capernaum, Decapolis, and Nazareth. They had gone to Jerusalem with Jesus to observe the Passover celebration, which had come and gone. They had no reason to be in Jerusalem. I don't even know if they packed enough clothes to be there for as long as they were. In fact, they didn't want to go to Jerusalem in the first place. They warned Jesus about going. But Jesus was so insistent that they decided to go with him. That assignment seemed to be over.

They did not feel at home or at ease in Jerusalem because they were followers of Jesus, who recently had been crucified. Since his crucifixion, they had been on edge from fear of those with strong anti-Jesus sentiment. They were worried about which one of them might be next. Even though Jesus was resurrected, he was talking about leaving them and going back to be with his Father in heaven. If Jesus was checking out of town, there really wasn't any reason for them to hang around. No one wants to stay where he or she does not feel at home.

It's also an unusual place because it is a place of bad memories: Jerusalem was the place of Judas's betrayal, Peter's denial, and everyone's cowardice and selfishness. It was the place where they failed to stand when Jesus needed them the most. It was the place where they saw the worst of themselves and the worst of each other. Who wants to stay in a place that reminds them of their failure? Who wants to stay in a place where they saw the worst in each other? Who wants to be reminded of the humiliation and shame?

Not only does Jesus tell them not to leave Jerusalem, but a few verses later he would tell them that their witnessing unto him must *begin* in Jerusalem. Even after they receive the promise from the Father, they can't go back home to Galilee to begin their work. They must begin the work in Jerusalem. It's an unusual place to stay and start.

When Jesus first called the apostles, he called them unto himself. He called them to be with him that he might send them. He called them first to himself and then to be sent out by him. Our calling is to the person of Christ, who then sends us to certain places. The place of assignment is not a matter of our picking. It's not a matter of our preference. It's not a matter of our penchant, partiality, or popularity—it's a matter of his purpose.

As the Lord who sets the policy, he also sets the place. Sometimes, the place is an unusual place, it's an unpopular place, it's an uncomfortable place. It's a place or situation that we'd never choose for ourselves and from which we would run away if we had the chance. It may be our job, our classroom, our neighborhood, our family or acquaintances where there is discomfort with us being a follower of Christ. It may be where none are in sync with the standards by which we live. It may be where opposition resides and seeks to thwart and hinder action and expression for Christ. It may be the place of the pain of our personal failings and faults.

As unusual as Jerusalem was, Jesus assigned them there. They didn't need to start where they weren't—they needed to start where they were, even if it was less than ideal for them. They needed to stay and start in Jerusalem. The place of the start is not the determiner of the success of the journey; a good start can happen in a bad place. Jesus can give fresh starts in the same place of failure. He can give fresh starts in the place of humiliation. He can give fresh starts in the place of disappointment. He can give fresh starts in the very headquarters of your enemies. After all, Jesus was resurrected in the same general area where he was crucified.

Part of the Lord's purpose was that they start where the enemy thought they were ended. Jesus would have them begin right where the enemy thought that they were stopped.

For some, your start is where the enemy thought that he stopped you. Your beginning is right where you thought it was your ending. The Lord can make the place of your worst defeat the launching pad of your greatest victory. It may not be the place of your picking or preference, but it is the place of his purpose. Babylon was not the place of Jeremiah and his generation's preference or picking, but it was the place of God's purpose. It was there that God told them to plant gardens, build homes, give and be given in marriage, multiply, and to seek the peace, because God knew the plans that he had for them, plans to prosper them and not to harm them, plans to give them a hope and a future (Jeremiah 29:11). It would be in that unusual place.

UNRELENTING PURPOSES, UNFAILING PROMISES

Jesus tells them to stay in Jerusalem for the promise of the Father. Jesus seeks to still them and embolden them by reminding them of the promise. Their journey with him had been about God fulfilling his promises; now, their remaining in Jerusalem is tied to another promise being fulfilled. This is no ordinary promise—this promise had been uttered by the prophet Joel centuries before them; it had been preached about by John the Baptist in the wilderness; Jesus had talked about it in the upper room. Now, Jesus is announcing that the promised power would be released to them as they obeyed him in an unusual place.

These unlikely people who are called to stay and to start in an unusual place are steadied by God's unrelenting purposes and unfailing promises. God's purpose for Jerusalem and for them was unrelenting and his promises were unfailing. Jeremiah 3:17 says, "At that time they will call Jerusalem The Throne of the LORD, and all nations will gather in Jerusalem to honor the name of the LORD. No longer will they follow the stubbornness of their evil hearts." There in Jerusalem would people from various nations come for the festival of Pentecost. There in Jerusalem would the Lord's promise of the Holy Spirit be fulfilled. There in Jerusalem, having been filled with the Holy Spirit, would they be heard speaking the wonderful works of God in the languages of the people from throughout the world. There would unlikely people in an unusual place experience the unrelenting purpose and unfailing promise of God.

The church is the body of believers who are steadied by the purposes and promises of God. The promises of the Lord stand sure. The purposes of the Lord are without fail. Such is the Lord's history.

He purposed and promised that Abraham and Sarah would become a great nation. He did not fail.

He purposed and promised that Joseph would ascend in prominence above his brothers and even his father. He did not fail.

He purposed and promised that a deliverer would come to lead Israel out of bondage. He did not fail.

He purposed and promised Moses that he would use Moses to lead them out, and that when they got out they would worship the Lord on his mountain. He did not fail.

He purposed and promised that Joshua would lead them across the Jordan and through Jericho to inherit the land that he promised Abraham. He did not fail.

He purposed and promised that an unknown and overlooked shepherd named David would become king over Israel in the place of Saul. He did not fail.

He purposed and promised to make an eternal house out of David, that from his line would come the One declared to be Wonderful, Counselor, Mighty God, Everlasting Father, and Prince of Peace. He did not fail.

He purposed and promised that he'd be born in Bethlehem. He did not fail. He purposed and promised that he'd be born to a virgin. He did not fail.

He purposed and promised that the seed of the serpent would bruise his heel and that he would bruise its head. He did not fail.

He purposed and promised that he'd be crucified on one day and raised on the third day. He did not fail.

He purposed and promised the coming of the Spirit in Jerusalem. He did not fail.

He purposed and promised the expansion of the church. He did not fail.

We are the body of believers who are steadied by the unrelenting purposes and unfailing promises of God.

5

A DIVINE ASSIGNMENT

In my former book, Theophilus, I wrote about all that Jesus began to do and to teach until the day he was taken up to heaven, after giving instructions through the Holy Spirit to the apostles he had chosen.
After his suffering, he presented himself to them and gave many convincing proofs that he was alive. He appeared to them over a period of forty days and spoke about the kingdom of God. On one occasion, while he was eating with them, he gave them this command: "Do not leave Jerusalem, but wait for the gift my Father promised, which you have heard me speak about. For John baptized with water, but in a few days you will be baptized with the Holy Spirit."

Then they gathered around him and asked him, "Lord, are you at this time going to restore the kingdom to Israel?"

He said to them: "It is not for you to know the times or dates the Father has set by his own authority. But you will receive power when the Holy Spirit comes on you; and you will be my witnesses in Jerusalem, and in all Judea and Samaria, and to the ends of the earth."

After he said this, he was taken up before their very eyes, and a cloud hid him from their sight.

They were looking intently up into the sky as he was going, when suddenly two men dressed in white stood beside them. "Men of Galilee," they said, "why do you stand here looking into the sky? This same Jesus, who has been taken from you into heaven, will come back in the same way you have seen him go into heaven." (Acts 1:1-11)

In the previous chapter, I shared with you the beginning of one of the post-resurrection/pre-ascension episodes that Jesus had with the apostles, where Jesus told them not to leave Jerusalem, but to wait for the promise of the Father. While John had baptized them with water, they would be baptized with the Holy Spirit. Together, we affirmed that the church is made up of unlikely people; that the church begins in and is constantly assigned to an unusual place; and that the church is steadied by the pursuit of God's unrelenting purposes and unfailing promises.

Under the direction of the Holy Spirit, I would write about the continuation of Jesus' work through the apostles and the church that God developed through them. As you read the book of Acts, you discover how God progressively revealed and led them to become the church of his intention. Their becoming the church was not one dramatic event or episode. It was a continual unfolding of divine purpose that is anchored upon and centered around God's redemptive and reconciling work in Jesus Christ.

Immediately upon Jesus' speaking about God fulfilling his promise by sending the Holy Spirit, the apostles' minds go down a road of their own making. They demonstrate the possibility of hearing a particular word from the Lord and taking that word down a road that the Lord never intended. With Jesus simply having told them to wait in Jerusalem for the promise of the Holy Spirit, the apostles' minds head down the road of the restoration of Israel to its former political glory and of their being in positions of authority. They have visions of ruling, reigning, exacting revenge on those who were dominating and oppressing them.

Jesus corrects them by saying that some things aren't for them to know. It's not for them to know the times or dates that the Father has set by his own authority. There are some things that are only reserved for the Father. They are not within the realm of our consideration. They are not within the purview of our concern. They solely and squarely belong to God.

In the times when our minds run down roads that are not God's intentions, God moves to correct us by letting us know what is not for us. Not every place that your mind travels is God's place for you. Some places singularly, solely, and squarely belong to God.

PNEUMATIC POWER

After letting them know what wasn't for them, Jesus then tells them what *is* for them. While it wasn't theirs to know the times or dates which the Father has set in his own authority, there is something for them to know. They would receive power when the Holy Spirit came on them, and they would be witnesses unto him.

Jesus alerts the apostles that *the church is pneumatic in power*. They would receive power. The word for power is *dynamis*. It speaks of dynamic power. We get our word *dynamite* from dynamis. It would be explosive power from the *Hagios Pneumatos*, Holy Spirit. They were to be a community that is pneumatically powered. Their power would not come from without, it would come from within them. This is resident power that inhabits them, influences them, and impels them; this would be purposeful and purpose-filled power. It's not the power for sitting on a throne, it's the power to fulfill the assignment given to them. Rather than the power of giving orders, it's the power to live under orders.

The power of the Holy Spirit is given to live under the orders of Christ and to fulfill the desires of Christ. That's why, right after telling them that they would receive power, Jesus says, "And you will be my witnesses." Their lives and service are to be unto him. Contact with Christ is to be their goal. Whatever they did was to be done with making contact with Christ in mind, both in terms of themselves and in terms of those to whom they witnessed.

EVANGELISTIC ASSIGNMENT

Not only is the church pneumatic in power, *the church is evangelistic in assignment.* The primary assignment of the church is to lead people in the making of contact with Christ. It is to bring people under the saving and sanctifying influence of Christ.

The power of the Holy Spirit is to enable the church to fulfill the assignment of witnessing, to be a *martys,* "one who has information of a given thing and who can give information concerning it." The task of the witness is to verify the truth of a claim, proposition, principle, or plan; it is to certify or validate. The call upon the first disciples and the call upon us is to bear witness to the truth of the claims of Jesus Christ. From us, people are to receive a message of certainty about Christ—they should be certain from us that Christ makes a difference. From us they should be certain that he is life, light, and love. From us they should be certain that he is the same yesterday, today, and forevermore. They should be certain that he is both faithful and just, compassionate and kind. It is with this realization that the hymn writer wrote, "Lift him up by living as a Christian ought. Let the world in you the Savior see. Then men will gladly follow him who once taught, 'I'll draw all men unto me.'"[1] Witnessing is not on the periphery of disciples' agendas, an add-on to an already crowded agenda. It is the core assignment.

With whom have you shared Jesus? To whom have you witnessed? Who is closer in contact with Jesus because of you? Who is more in love with Jesus because of you?

This call to witness is the call to certify the truth by our death. A true witness is one who can verify the truth by his or her willingness to die. Throughout the world, men and women who confess Christ verify the truth of their claim by a willingness to die. We in the United States are insulated from those encounters. Yet, they are very real and more frequent than what is reported by any media outlet. Consider statistics provided by Open Doors: Each month, 491 Christians are killed for their faith; 425 churches and Christian properties are attacked; 397 believers are detained without trial, arrested, sentenced, or imprisoned, and 319 Christians are abducted for faith-related reasons.[2] As people endure such, they certify the truth of their witness by their willingness to suffer and die.

While that degree of suffering has yet to reach our shores, there is a subtle push within our society to marginalize the name of Jesus. Those who are filled with the Holy Spirit are given power to bear witness in the face of the attempts to marginalize and minimize his name.

Further, being a true witness is not just verifying the truth of Christ by the death *of* us, but also by there being a death *in* us. We verify the truth of the life-changing power of Christ by some things no longer being alive in us. Paul writes in Romans 8:10-13:

> But if Christ is in you, then even though your body is subject to death because of sin, the Spirit gives life because of righteousness. And if the Spirit of him who raised Jesus from the dead is living in you, he who raised Christ from the dead will also give life to your mortal bodies because of his Spirit who lives in you.
>
> Therefore, brothers and sisters, we have an obligation—but it is not to the flesh, to live according to it. For if you live according to the flesh, you will die; but if by the Spirit you put to death the misdeeds of the body, you will live.

And in Galatians, Paul writes, "I have been crucified with Christ and I no longer live, but Christ lives in me. The life I now live in the body, I live by faith in the Son of God, who loved me and gave himself for me" (Galatians 2:20).

The call to be witnesses is the call to verify the truth through death. Could it be that the world questions the truth of our witness because it sees so little death in us to verify our claims? Could it be that our unwillingness to die to self has severely hampered the power of our witness? Could it be that because we gossip and backbite just as much, lie and cheat just as much, shack up and tip out just as much, the certainty of our witness is called into question? Could the low view that the society has of the church and those who make up the church be because too many of us have been false witnesses by our actions; false witnesses by our attitudes; false witnesses by our responses? For our witness to be seen as true, there must be some death in us that verifies the truth of our claim. Some things that were alive before we met Christ should have died in us after we met him. Some things ought to be in the cemetery. Some stuff ought to be in the morgue. Some things that haven't died, at least ought to be in intensive care on a respirator with Holy Ghost telling us to pull the plug.

EXPANSIVE MOVEMENT

Jesus continues with the words, "And you will be my witnesses in Jerusalem, and in all Judea and Samaria, and to the ends of the earth" (Acts 1:8). Jesus gives an outline of their movement. The outline that he gives reveals something else about the church. *The church is progressively expansive in its movement.* Having told them to stay in Jerusalem, Jesus now tells them to start in Jerusalem. They are told to start where they are, even if it isn't where they imagined starting. We may imagine our start being somewhere other than where we are. That's our imagination, not God's plan. God is calling for us to let go of our imagined place, to start working in God's assigned place, and to start watching God do what God wants to do with us. The place of our start is simply that; the place of our start. The work of God in our life is progressively expansive.

While the disciples would start in Jerusalem, they would not be limited to Jerusalem. They were to move from Jerusalem to Judea, the place where they were looked down on and not believed to be as religious. It's the territory where they weren't easily accepted and would have to prove themselves. But they wouldn't be limited to Judea; they were to go to Samaria. This was the region of traditional rivalry and hostility, it's the place of ethnic and racial tension that went back generations and had its roots during the time of the Assyrian invasion as well as the return from the Babylonian exile. They were called to go to where they would normally avoid.

With the woman at the well, Jesus crossed the barrier of race and gender, speaking to her about living water being available to her. As a result, she witnessed and brought salvation to a town (John 4:1-42). The call to go into Samaria is a particular challenge for the North American church. The call to bridge historical racial, ethnic, and gender barriers is a call that all too often is ignored; we jump over Samaria and go to the uttermost parts of the earth. We lift relationships that we have overseas, while neglecting relational development across town.

Just as Jesus challenged these early followers to refuse to allow their cultural context to limit, restrict, or excuse them from their call to move across race and ethnicity, so does Jesus challenge us to refuse to allow our context to restrict us to witnessing to those of our own race. We are challenged to overcome racial and ethnic hostility with the gospel of Jesus Christ. Part of this means seeing Christ as our pain bearer as well as our sin bearer. The overcoming of the pain inherent within our context has been born by Jesus, and he offers us his peace to thrust us into reconciliation.

We are called to step into the cultural realities of others and bring them the gospel. Indeed the gospel is transcultural. It applies to a universal problem, that results in a universal need, that offers a universal solution and Savior.

EXPANSIVE POWER IN HIS NAME

But they weren't limited to Samaria. Jesus then told them to be his witnesses to the ends of the earth. This is where they are not known and have never been. It's the realm of the unknown, the unpredictable, and the uncertain; it is the territory of the strange and the foreign. Language and customs are different; means, manners, and mores are different.

We are called to be progressively expansive in our movement. It is the call beyond what is, who is, where is, and how is, and into what we've never seen, who we've never met, where we've never been, and how it's never been done. It is the call to progressively expansive movement that extends to the ends of the earth. No distance is too far, you can never go far enough. No effort is too much, you can never do too much for him. No amount of people is too many, you can never reach too many people for him.

The disciples were called to go where they had never gone before, to people whom they'd never seen before, who spoke languages that they'd never spoken before. It was an expansive challenge and call. They were called to understand that the matter was not people knowing them; the matter was people coming to know Jesus. Their names had no power, the power was in his name: Salvation was in his name. Redemption was in his name. Forgiveness was in his name. Healing was in his name. Deliverance was in his name. Breakthrough was in his name. His name would be good in Jerusalem. His name would be good in Judea. His name would be good in Samaria. It would be good in Ethiopia. His name would be good in the uttermost parts of the earth.

History bears witness that the power of his name has been found and felt in every place. It had power in Antioch, in Salamis, in Paphos, in Antioch of Pisidia, in Iconium, in Lystra, in Derbe, in Macedonia, in Philippi, in Thessalonica, in Berea, in Athens, in Corinth, in Ephesus, in Colossae, in Rome, in Constantinople, in Egypt, in Britain, in Germany, in India, in Spain, in France, in China, in the Caribbean, in the United States; throughout Africa, Asia, Latin America. There is power in his name. I found out that there is power in his name in Jackson, Mississippi; Atlanta, Georgia; Pittsburgh, Pennsylvania; Charlotte, North Carolina; Cape Town, South Africa. Wherever we take the name of Jesus, the name has power. In the hood, it has power. In the country, it has power. In the suburbs, it has power.

PROPELLED BY EXPECTATION

There is one more thing about the church from this encounter: *The church is propelled by an extraordinary expectation.* Having spoken to them for the very last time, Jesus begins to ascend into heaven. As Jesus ascended into heaven, there were two men in white apparel who said, "Men of Galilee, . . . why do you stand here looking into the sky? This same Jesus, who has been taken from you into heaven will come back in the same way that you have seen him go into heaven" (Acts 1:11). They were assured that Jesus was coming back.

Jesus had told them, "I am going there to prepare a place for you . . . And if I go and prepare a place for you, I will come back and take you to be with me that you also may be where I am" (John 14:2-3). Jesus was coming back. They wanted to be ready when he returned; they didn't want to be caught with their work undone. They preached in expectation. They witnessed in expectation. They suffered in expectation. They endured in expectation. They sacrificed in expectation. They journeyed in expectation. John got a revelation of a new heaven and a new earth; he saw the Holy City coming down from God as a bride adorned for her husband. It wasn't the new Rome, Ephesus, Corinth, or Athens—it was new Jerusalem.

We have an extraordinary expectation. The Lord shall return and we will be called to meet him. In my younger years, this expectation didn't hold a lot of excitement for me. But now that I have some years behind me and some experiences under me, I better understand the excitement of over there. I better understand the hope of over there, where the wicked will cease from troubling and the weary will be at rest. Over there, where there is no more crying, no more dying, no more sickness, no more pain, no more tears.

That's our motivation for our divine assignment—the Lord is coming back, he's soon to return. "For the Lord himself will come down from heaven, with a loud command, with the voice of the archangel and with the trumpet call of God, and the dead in Christ will rise first. After that, we who are still alive and are left will be caught up together with them in the clouds to meet the Lord in the air" (1 Thessalonians 4:16-17). He is coming back. Then we'll join the saints of the ages in the new Jerusalem. Then we'll join the number that no man can number, made up of every nation, every tribe, every kindred, every clan. And every tongue, every language shall sing together in one language to him who sits on the throne, and unto the Lamb, "Praise and honor and glory and power, for ever and ever!" (Revelation 5:13). Salvation and glory and power belong to our God—hallelujah! For our Lord God Almighty reigns. Let us rejoice and be glad and give him glory.

6

EMPOWERED TO PROCLAIM

When the Day of Pentecost had fully come, they were all with one accord in one place. And suddenly there came a sound from heaven, as of a rushing mighty wind, and it filled the whole house where they were sitting. Then there appeared to them divided tongues, as of fire, and one sat upon each of them. And they were all filled with the Holy Spirit and began to speak with other tongues, as the Spirit gave them utterance.

And there were dwelling in Jerusalem Jews, devout men, from every nation under heaven. And when this sound occurred, the multitude came together, and were confused, because everyone heard them speak in his own language. Then they were all amazed and marveled, saying to one another, "Look, are not all these who speak Galileans? And how is it that we hear, each in our own language in which we were born? . . . We hear them speaking in our own tongues the wonderful works of God." So they were all amazed and perplexed, saying to one another, "Whatever could this mean?"

Others mocking said, "They are full of new wine."

But Peter, standing up with the eleven, raised his voice and said to them, "Men of Judea and all who dwell in Jerusalem, let this be known to you, and heed my words. For these are not drunk, as you suppose, since it is only the third hour of the day. But this is what was spoken by the prophet Joel:

'And it shall come to pass in the last days, says God,
That I will pour out of My Spirit on all flesh;
Your sons and your daughters shall prophesy,
Your young men shall see visions,
Your old men shall dream dreams.
And on My menservants and on My maidservants
I will pour out My Spirit in those days;
And they shall prophesy.
I will show wonders in heaven above.
And signs in the earth beneath:
Blood and fire and vapor of smoke.
The sun shall be turned into darkness,
And the moon into blood,
Before the coming of the great and awesome day of
  the LORD.
And it shall come to pass
That whoever calls on the name of the LORD
shall be saved.'

"Men of Israel, hear these words: Jesus of Nazareth, a Man attested by God to you by miracles, wonders, and signs which God did through Him in your midst, as you yourselves also know—Him, being delivered by the determined purpose and foreknowledge of God, you have taken by lawless hands, have crucified, and put to death; whom God raised up, having loosed the pains of death, because it was not possible that He should be held by it. . . . This Jesus God has raised up, of which we are all witnesses. Therefore being exalted to the right hand of God, and having received from the Father the promise of the Holy Spirit, He poured out this which you now see and hear. . . . Therefore let all the house of Israel know assuredly that God has made this Jesus, whom you crucified, both Lord and Christ."

Now when they heard this, they were cut to the heart, and said to Peter and the rest of the apostles, "Men and brethren, what shall we do?"

Then Peter said to them, "Repent, and let every one of you be baptized in the name of Jesus Christ for the remission of sins; and you shall receive the gift of the Holy Spirit. For the promise is to you and to your children, and to all who are afar off, as many as the Lord our God will call."

And with many other words he testified and exhorted them, saying, "Be saved from this perverse generation."

Then those who gladly received his word were baptized; and that day about three thousand souls were added to them. (Acts 2:1-41 NKJV)

With the instructions from and ascension of Jesus, the apostles assume an active, expectant posture. Having been told not to leave Jerusalem and to start being witnesses in Jerusalem, they remain in Jerusalem and spend time together in prayer. Jesus had taught them to pray. One of the last things that he told them prior to his being betrayed and crucified was that they should pray and not faint lest they enter into temptation (Matthew 26:41; Luke 18:1).

Therefore, they prayed. Prayer would be their constant characteristic, it was the lifeline of their unity. During their three years together with Jesus, Jesus was the point of their unity. They were held together by his physical presence. Now, in the wake of Jesus' physical absence, they sought his spiritual presence through prayer. He had told them in Matthew 18:19-20, "Again, truly I tell you that if two of you on earth agree about anything they ask for, it will be done for them by my Father in heaven. For where two or three gather in my name, there am I with them." Fueled by prayer, the apostles selected a replacement for Judas named Matthias. Prayer would bind them closer together through strengthening their sense of Jesus. Prayer would embolden them to continue together in Jesus and for Jesus. Prayer would be the channel through which Jesus would direct them.

The church is the community whose unity and life are sustained through prayer. It is through praying together that the presence of Christ is promised to be profoundly felt.

The unity of the church is around Christ and his presence. That sense of oneness is sustained through an agreement that happens in prayer.

EMPOWERED AT PENTECOST

Acts 2 opens with the arrival of the feast day of Pentecost. This festival was instituted to commemorate God's giving the law at Mount Sinai, which was accompanied by thunder and lightning. It was also known as the Feast of the Harvest. It was the feast day when the people would present an offering of new grain to the Lord. Persons from every nation were in Jerusalem for this festival.

Again the disciples were in the upper room praying. Suddenly, a sound that comes from heaven as of a rushing and mighty wind fills the place. Cloven tongues of fire appear above each person's head as they each are filled with the Holy Spirit. They begin to speak in other tongues as the Spirit of God gives utterance. There is a release of supernatural ability, which at the time they don't fully understand. They begin to speak in languages unknown to them, but known to others. It will not make sense to them until they come into contact with the people for whom the ability is meant.

There are some things that God does with us and within us that don't make sense to us at the time, because it's not done for us—it's done for people whom God wants to impact that we have yet to meet. There are gifts and graces that God bestows with which we may not know what to do—we may feel awkward, weird, or out of place when God bestows, because those for whom it is needed or intended have yet to arrive. When God is active in the pursuit of his purpose, things that God does may not make sense now, but they will make sense later.

In the midst of this supernatural empowerment, some people who had been in Jerusalem for the festival hear the rumblings going on in the upper room. They are drawn to see what's going on. When they arrive, they are taken aback by what they hear. What they hear doesn't line up with what they see. They see Galileans, who are supposedly illiterate and irreligious, speaking the wonderful works of God in their own languages. God produces a reversal of the tower of Babel. At Babel, the people were all of one language and God confused their languages and scattered them. Here, God brings people of different languages together and gives the disciples the ability to speak to them in their language. This is the beginning of God gathering what God scattered. On the feast day that celebrates the harvest and the ingathering, God presents the opportunity for them to engage and to gather a harvest of souls.

With God setting in motion such a profound move, the people respond in two unique ways; curiosity and sarcasm. One group asks, "What does it mean?" Another says, "They are drunk." The questioners are not worldly heathens, these are God-fearing Jews who are versed in the Law and knowledgeable of the prophets. Yet, they don't know what to make of this new thing that God is doing. Hence, they seek to make light of, to minimize, to denounce.

From its very inception, there are those who, being religious, don't get the church. On the day of its birth, the church is both not understood and misunderstood. From that moment until now, the church has constantly had to defend and to explain itself. With people either simply not understanding the church or being intent on negatively defining and characterizing the church, the church has lived and thrived. Wherever the gospel has been preached and believed, causing people to come together in covenant fellowship, there have been those who don't get it and who don't want it.

At the point of its birth, while yet an infant, the church is met with a crisis. Peter steps up to the plate, realizing that God's work can be best interpreted and explained by himself and the other eleven. With others dismissing, disregarding, and denigrating the church, Peter steps up to defend and to explain.

In our day and age, when so many are quick to write off the church, dismiss the church, and even denigrate the church, there must be some who are willing to stand to defend and explain the church. We must heed the words that Peter would write later:

Who is going to harm you if you are eager to do good? But even if you should suffer for what is right, you are blessed. "Do not fear their threats; do not be frightened." But in your hearts revere Christ as Lord. Always be prepared to give an answer to everyone who asks you to give the reason for the hope that you have. But do this with gentleness and respect. (1 Peter 3:13-15)

GOD KEEPS HIS WORD

There are four parts to Peter's defense. First, *the church is the body that asserts that God keeps his word.* Peter begins with the words,

These people are not drunk. . . . It's only nine in the morning! No this is what was spoken by the prophet Joel:

"In the last days, God says, I will pour out my Spirit on all people. Your sons and daughters will prophesy, your young men will see visions, your old men will dream dreams. Even on my servants, both men and women, I will pour out my Spirit in those days, and they will prophesy. I will show wonders in the heavens above and signs on the earth below, blood and fire and billows of smoke. The sun will be turned to darkness and the moon to blood before the coming of the great and glorious day of the Lord." (Acts 2:15-20)

Hundreds of years had passed between the time of Joel's utterance and God's fulfillment. In the course of that time,

Jesus was born, grew up, was crucified, buried, resurrected from the dead, and ascended into heaven. Then after all of that, God fulfilled his promise by sending the Holy Spirit. Though it took a while, God kept his word. Though many things happened in between promise and fulfillment, God kept his word. God did just what God said that God would do. The darkest of moments did not stop God from keeping God's word.

The church is the body that boldly declares that God keeps God's word. God can be trusted to do exactly what God says that God will do. Time may elapse; people may come and go; tears may flow; darkness may appear—but God keeps his word. Hell may play its best hand and the enemy may celebrate too early, but God keeps his word. Some words of God are seen fulfilled by the generation in which they were spoken, and some are seen fulfilled by generations that succeed the initial hearers. The faithfulness of God is not in who sees the fulfillment—it's in God fulfilling the word. There are some promises that my grandparents never saw fulfilled; I have seen them fulfilled. There are some promises that I have heard, that I may never see fulfilled; there is a generation after me that will see it. It's not about the generation that hears or sees the promise, it's the God who makes and keeps the promise.

BY THE POWER OF THE SPIRIT

There is another matter that Peter wants them to understand. What they are seeing is an indication that the church operates out of a different source and level of authority and influence. *The church operates by the power of the Holy Spirit.*

Prior to Pentecost, the Law was the source of authority and influence, the letter was the level of authority. Those who were in Jerusalem had come in response to the legislated festival celebration. The one hundred and twenty were in the upper room fasting and praying. Jesus had promised them power from on high by way of the Holy Spirit. At Pentecost, with the sending of the Holy Spirit, God established a new source and level of authority and influence. It was no longer what was written on paper, but it was what is written on the heart by way of the Spirit.

Notice that when God did this, the people were called "drunk." Another term for drunk is *under the influence*. They were not under the influence of wine, they were under the influence of something greater than wine. They were under the influence of the Holy Spirit. This was a new source and level of authority and influence. It was no longer statements external to them, it was spirit internal to them. The Law operated from the outside in, the Spirit operates from the inside out. The letter kills, but the Spirit gives life. God was establishing another level of authority and influence.

The church operates by the power of the Holy Spirit. The Spirit is the primary influencer. The Spirit establishes even greater levels of authority and influence. God empowered them to do what they had never done before. They spoke in every known language of the people of the world. Having spoken a broken version of Aramaic for all of their lives, the Holy Spirit broadens their language base to that of Parthian, Mede, Arabic, Latin, and others.

This new level of authority and influence was for a new level of call and accountability. They were called to a global work and a global accountability. By way of the Holy Spirit, God equipped the people to rise up to the level of calling and accountability that God placed on them. Having called them to the people of the world, God gave them an ability to speak in a way that the people of the world could understand.

To those with a narrow frame of reference, Peter alerts them (and us) to God stretching some things—God is spreading some things out. God's desired impact is beyond them. Likewise, God's call and claim on us goes beyond our walls. By way of the Holy Spirit, God gives us a supernatural endowment to accept the call and pursue the claim of God wherever it leads. It's beyond one's race or ethnicity. God's claim goes beyond our hometown; it's for the world. New and broader places require a broader level of authority and influence. God bringing the people from around the world to the upper room is an indication of what that power is for and where the disciples are to go.

We must pay attention to whom God brings into the space of our lives. Often there is an assignment with their arrival. Often God is indicating a direction that he has for us. Often God is indicating the rhyme and reason for the ability, the grace, the experiences and exposures that he's bestowed upon us and where he wants to expand his influence. When God wants to use us to expand his influence, it often means that he must stretch us. He must stretch our comfort zone. He must stretch our preconceived notions. The power of the Holy Spirit is to equip us to stretch to expand his influence in the world.

CALLED TO PROPHETIC ACTION

Peter continues with yet a third thing for them to understand about the church: *The church is the community called to prophetic action based upon expanded perceptions and enlarged perspectives.* Peter quotes the prophet Joel:

"In the last days, God says, I will pour out my Spirit on all people. Your sons and daughters will prophesy, your young men will see visions, your old men will dream dreams. Even on my servants, both men and women, I will pour out my Spirit in those days, and they will prophesy." (Acts 2: 17-18)

With Pentecost, God set in motion a heightened level of sight and speech. God established a heightened level of sight through visions and dreams. With eyes wide open, God would communicate through visions—God-enhanced and God-expanded vision. They wouldn't just see, they would see into what they were seeing. They would have a pro-seeing, an ability not just to see deeply, but also to see distantly; they would be able to see purpose. Young men would see visions, while older men would dream dreams. They would have an alternative consciousness. They would not simply see things as they are, but also as they can be and should be.

Sons and daughters would prophesy, would speak forth the word of God. The characteristic speech of sons and daughters would be prophetic. Prior to Pentecost, there were schools of prophets. Before, the spirit of prophecy would come upon the elders of Israel that were appointed to government. But now, the Spirit would be poured out upon all persons regardless of rank or gender.[1] Sons and daughters, owners and servants, through the Holy Spirit, are empowered to speak forth God's word.

The church is the body endowed by the Holy Spirit to see and speak prophetically due to enhanced vision and understanding. From the church, the world should be challenged and critiqued because of a deeper level of insight and understanding. We are called not just to see, but to see into. Not just to see what is, but also to see what can be and what should be by the will and power of God. There is a word that God is putting into the hearts and mouths of God's people that must be proclaimed.

THE CENTRALITY OF JESUS

Finally, *the church is the community whose central and primary point of witness is Jesus.* Having provided an explanation and defense for what the people had just seen, Peter shifts gears and begins to talk about Jesus. He reminds them that Jesus was recognized for doing miracles and performing signs and wonders. While they thought that they were taking Jesus by force, God actually handed Jesus over to them, and Jesus allowed himself to be taken in order that God's set purpose might be fulfilled. Wicked men nailed Jesus to the cross, but God raised him from the dead and has exalted him to the right hand of his throne so that their sin could be forgiven. If they called on that name, they'd be saved. There is salvation through Jesus Christ.

The name of Jesus is the name by which we are saved. When the people heard the noise from the outside at Pentecost, it was so that they would be curious enough to come into the room. When they came into the room and heard the disciples speaking the words of God in their own language, it set the stage for a conversation about the faithfulness of God. The conversation about the faithfulness of God always ends up with Jesus. It all points to Jesus: Born of the Virgin Mary, suffered under Pontius Pilate, was crucified, dead, and buried, descended into hell, preached to the spirits held captive, on the third day he rose again from the dead, ascended into heaven, and sits at the right hand of God the Father. And he is soon to return.

They preached Jesus. They taught Jesus. They prayed in the name of Jesus. They healed in his name. They suffered for his name. They were jailed because of his name. They braved the sea, shipwrecks, stoning, hunger, cold, and nakedness, all for the name of Jesus.

Here we are nearly two thousand years later with the same assertion. He is the central and primary point of our witness. Everything that we do points to Jesus. The teaching points to Jesus. The counseling points to Jesus. The mentoring points to Jesus. The hosting points to Jesus. The feeding points to Jesus. The caring points to Jesus. The fellowship points to Jesus. The life that we have points to Jesus. The joy that we have points to Jesus. The peace that we have points to Jesus. The strength that we have points to Jesus. The calm that we have points to Jesus. This is our power to proclaim.

7

A COMMUNITY OF COMMITMENTS

"Therefore let all Israel be assured of this: God has made this Jesus, whom you crucified, both Lord and Messiah."

When the people heard this, they were cut to the heart and said to Peter and the other apostles, "Brothers, what shall we do?"

Peter replied, "Repent and be baptized, every one of you, in the name of Jesus Christ for the forgiveness of your sins. And you will receive the gift of the Holy Spirit. The promise is for you and your children and for all who are far off—for all whom the Lord our God will call."

With many other words he warned them; and he pleaded with them, "Save yourselves from this corrupt generation." Those who accepted his message were baptized, and about three thousand were added to their number that day.

They devoted themselves to the apostles' teaching and to fellowship, to the breaking of bread and to prayer. Everyone was filled with awe at the many wonders and signs performed by the apostles. All the believers were together and had everything in common. They sold property and possessions to give to anyone who had need. Every day they continued to meet together in the temple courts. They broke bread in their homes and ate together with glad and sincere hearts, praising God and enjoying the favor of all the people. And the Lord added to their number daily those who were being saved. (Acts 2:36-47)

We have been on a journey designed to reacquaint some and to introduce others to a biblical understanding of the nature and purpose of the church. There is a need for us to get the church—to have an appreciation of what God has established for the redemption of the world. The church is God's idea for believers to grow in Christlikeness and to represent him to a needy world.

Our journey has taken us along the course of God developing disciples from followers of Jesus and into the beginning of the church. Theirs was a developmental process of becoming what God has in mind in terms of being the church.

When we looked at the day of Pentecost in chapter six, we learned that the church is the community whose life and unity are sustained through prayer. It is the body that boldly declares that God keeps his word and that operates out of a different source and level of authority and influence. It is the fellowship of believers who are called to prophetic action based on expanded perceptions and perspectives. It is the gathering of those whose central and primary point of witness is Jesus.

Peter proclaims Jesus, and three thousand souls are saved on that day. Having accepted Christ, they are baptized. Through baptism, they identify themselves as members of the family of God. They are a part of a new community, the believers in the Lord Jesus Christ. Luke informs us that God adds them to the church. Having believed and been baptized, they are not left to fend for themselves or exist on their own unto themselves. They are added to the church. Their growth in Christlikeness and their witness to the world would not be by themselves. It would be in the context of belonging to the church. They are a part of a new community, the believers in the Lord Jesus Christ.

As a part of this new community, they are identified as devoting themselves to the apostles' teaching and to the fellowship, to the breaking of the bread, and to prayer. "All the believers were together and had everything in common." They gave to anyone who had need. They met together daily in the temple courts. "They broke bread in their homes and ate together with glad and sincere hearts" (Acts 2:44-46). This is the very nature and heart of the church. Authentic life in Christ is not lived in the context of isolation. Authentic life in Christ is lived in the context of commitment to growth in Christ in relationship and community with other believers. *The church is the place where we collectively carry out vital commitments.* Luke says that they devoted themselves; this is their shared action. They also had several shared commitments we can find.

COMMITTED TO THE WORD OF GOD

The first shared commitment is the apostles' doctrine—the word of God. The foundation upon which they would stand as a community was the word of God. Jesus said, "If you hold to my teaching, you are really my disciples. Then you will know the truth, and the truth will set you free" (John 8:31-32).

We carry out our commitment to sound doctrine and the word. The foundation upon which we as believers stand is still the word of God. The word of God is the center of our lives as believers. The centrality of the Word is reflected in the psalmist declaring,

> Blessed is the one
> who does not walk in step with the wicked
> or stand in the way that sinners take
> or sit in the company of mockers,
> but whose delight is in the law of the LORD,
> and who meditates on his law day and night.
> (Psalm 1:1-2)

It is reflected in the words, "Your word I have hidden in my heart, That I might not sin against You" (Psalm 119:11 NKJV).

It is the Word that is able to order our steps along the paths that God has ordained for us. It is the Word that builds the faith to believe. It is the Word that instructs us in righteousness. It is the Word that convicts us of sin. It is the Word that encourages us and enlivens our hope in God. *The church is the place where we carry out our shared commitment to the word of God.*

COMMITTED TO FELLOWSHIP

The second commitment is the commitment to fellowship. Those that believed came and joined the disciples. They attached themselves. They connected themselves. They weren't spectating attendees—they became a part of the body of believers. They invested themselves personally. Relationship and community could only occur by them personally investing themselves into the lives of others. In so doing, they became accountable to someone, indeed to the whole body.

Herein is an indictment of the current way in which many relate to the church. There are those who can attend a church for five years and never make a commitment or connection to the church. What is expressed is a desire to remain unaccountable. Lack of spiritual accountability may be comfortable, but it is not Christian. Authentic Christianity is relational. Genuine relationship requires not just knowing but being known and being held accountable. This by nature necessitates connection, attachment, and commitment. *The church is the place where we carry out our shared commitment to fellowship.*

These new converts joined the other believers and committed to fellowship. Every day they continued to meet together in the temple courts. Their commonness in Christ was affirmed. Their oneness in the Spirit was celebrated. Their unity in the faith was observed. They went from house to house in fellowship. As they shared together, they were accountable to and for each other. Whenever anyone had need, their needs were met by the fellowship.

Let me be clear. The worship service is not designed for relationship and community building. Community is built in a much smaller group of two, three, eight, ten, or twelve. It's built in a life group, a Sunday school class, a ministry, and a Bible study group.

Fellowship occurs when we bring ourselves into a place of intentionally relating with others based on the commonality that we have in Christ and the kingdom. It is through fellowship that we fulfill the call to admonish one another, to edify one another, to encourage one another, to exhort one another, to love one another, and to bear one another's burdens. This can only occur through attachment and connection.

It's in the fellowship that we discover that we are not alone in the struggle. It's in the fellowship that we learn that there is no temptation that is not common to man. It's in the fellowship that we can receive a witness that God is able, that God can make a way, and that God will see us through. In the fellowship, someone will tell us that we can make it and that we are somebody because we are a child of God. In the fellowship, someone can tell us, "Been there, done that. I'm not going back." Through the fellowship, we realize that we're not alone and that we don't have to face what we face by ourselves. There are those who will be with us; there are those who will pray for us.

COMMITTED TO THE LORD'S SUPPER AND THE CROSS

The apostles and early converts also committed themselves to the Lord's Supper and to Calvary. The family of God has always been identified as being devoted to the breaking of the bread, or the common meal. This isn't about Sunday dinner, this is referring to the observance of the Lord's Supper. We do so out of obedience to the command of Christ. While Jesus never told his disciples to observe his birth, he did tell them to observe his death. He did tell them to remember his broken body and his shed blood. He wanted them to remember the depth of his love for them and the extent of his obedience to the Father. He wanted them to know the high cost that God places on their redemption.

Jesus did this because he knew that we are prone to slip into falsity if we forget the cost of our salvation. When we stare at the cross and see a bloodied Jesus suffering for us, we can't help but be grateful to God for so great a love and so great a sacrifice. When we take the bread and the cup, we are reminded of the amazing grace of God. As a result, we can't help but serve God because we're reminded that we're not our own; we belong to God. We've been redeemed. We've been purchased of God. We've been bought with a price. Therefore, we are to serve God with our body. Our life is to be an offering of gratitude for the radical love of God for us.

The church is the place where we carry out our shared commitment to the Lord's Supper and to Calvary. Every time the bread and the cup are offered, I can't help but show up because I see that Jesus was broken for my brokenness and that his blood was shed to cleanse me, purge me, purchase me, and release me. The breaking of the bread reminds me of where I should have been and of what should have happened to me, but God laid on Jesus the iniquity of us all. He was wounded for our transgressions, bruised for our iniquity, the chastisement of our peace was upon him, and by his stripes we are healed (Isaiah 53:5-6).

COMMITTED TO PRAYER

The next shared commitment is the commitment to prayer. The early believers committed themselves to prayer. They were identified and shaped by their communication with God. They were a praying people. Their connection to God and with God helped keep them within the will of God. As followers of Jesus, they observed his lifestyle of prayer: He led a devotional life. He maintained openness to the Father and what the Father had in mind. His prayer life demonstrated his reliance on the Father for guidance and power. Before every major move, there was prayer time with the Father. After every move, there was prayer time with the Father.

So impressed were the disciples by Jesus' prayer life that they asked Jesus to teach them to pray. Jesus taught them the model prayer (Matthew 6:9-13). He encouraged them to always pray and not give up (Luke 18:1), to pray believing that the Father knows what they need before they ask (Matthew 6:8), and to watch as well as pray lest they enter into temptation (Mark 14:38).

Jesus was devoted to prayer, his ability to please God was strengthened by prayer. Therefore, the church committed itself to prayer. Prayer influenced the quality of their relationships and community. Prior to Pentecost, they committed to prayer. When threatened by the Sanhedrin, they committed to prayer. When James was killed and Peter was imprisoned, they committed to prayer. Through prayer, God was able to show himself faithful. They gained direction and boldness.

God calls us to be devoted to prayer as a community of faith. Through prayer we relinquish self-concern and are open to receiving God's will. Through prayer, God is able to release his power. There is an exponential move that God desires to make among us and within us. The channel through which God is able to move is prayer. *The church is the place where we carry out our shared commitment to prayer.*

COMMITTED TO JOY

They were committed to demonstrable joy. The community of the people of God was known for its joy. Acts 2:46-47 reads, "They broke bread in their homes and ate together with glad and sincere hearts, praising God and enjoying the favor of all the people. And the Lord added to their number daily those who were being saved." As families of faith, they celebrated their joy in the Lord. They praised God. They blessed God. They magnified God. They expressed their feelings about God. They were glad about God and happy in Jesus.

Their joy in the Lord translated into their joy in each other. They were seasoned with joy. This joy caught the eyes of the casual observer. It caused them to garner the favor of others. Others couldn't help but be positive about them because of the joy and gladness that they had in each other and in God. A great witness was lifted to the world by the way in which they enjoyed relationship and community. In them, the world saw what it had been looking for and was missing.

To them, the Lord added daily. Where God saw authentic relationship and community, God added daily. Where God saw devotion to the Word, to fellowship, to the Lord's Supper, and to prayer, God added daily. Where God saw joy and gladness in him and in each other, God added daily. Where God received praise, blessing, glory, and honor, God added daily.

How could they not be glad in God and happy in Jesus? When you consider all that they had seen for themselves, how could they not be glad in God and happy in Jesus? How could they not praise God? After having seen Jesus turn water into wine, tell the waters to be still, walk on water, heal the sick, feed five thousand with a small lunch, raise the dead three times, be crucified for their sins on Friday and be raised from the dead on Sunday morning, how could they not praise God? They had to give God praise.

The church is the body where we carry out the shared commitment to demonstrable joy. When we think of who God is, how good God has been to us, and what God has done for us, we can't help but be glad in him. We can't help but praise him. As good as God has been to us, we can't help but praise his name. We want to give him the highest praise for being refuge and strength, for being light and salvation, for being a mighty fortress and strong tower, for being a deliverer and a healer.

I'm glad in God and happy in Jesus. I'm glad that he's kept me alive. I'm glad that he's protected me. I'm glad that he loves me. I'm glad that he cares for me. I'm glad that he sent Jesus to die for me. I'm happy in Jesus' obedience; I'm happy in Jesus' sacrifice; I'm happy in Jesus' blood; I'm happy in Jesus' resurrection. I'm glad in God and happy in Jesus. I'm glad that I belong to God. I'm glad that I've been delivered. I'm glad that I've been set free. I'm glad that I've been placed into the family of God. I'm glad that I've been added to the family.

8

TRANSFORMED BY JESUS

THE LAME MAN AT THE TEMPLE

One day Peter and John were going up to the temple at the time of prayer—at three in the afternoon. Now a man who was lame from birth was being carried to the temple gate called Beautiful, where he was put every day to beg from those going into the temple courts. When he saw Peter and John about to enter, he asked them for money. Peter looked straight at him, as did John. Then Peter said, "Look at us!" So the man gave them his attention, expecting to get something from them.

Then Peter said, "Silver or gold I do not have, but what I do have I give you. In the name of Jesus Christ of Nazareth, walk." Taking him by the right hand, he helped him up, and instantly the man's feet and ankles became strong. He jumped to his feet and began to walk. Then he went with them into the temple courts, walking and jumping, and praising God. When all the people saw him walking and praising God, they recognized him as the same man who used to sit begging at the temple gate called Beautiful, and they

> were filled with wonder and amazement at what had happened to him.
>
> While the man held on to Peter and John, all the people were astonished and came running to them in the place called Solomon's Colonnade. (Acts 3:1-11)

For years I was relegated to life on the margins. My place was that of the periphery. My lot was that of dependence due to disability. The initial years were somewhat tough. But over time, I had begun to accept it as my lot. I adapted to it. I made accommodations for it. In fact, I developed a structured system to accommodate for my lot. Every day, I was placed at one of the gates that led to the temple, where I would beg for alms. Back in the day, there was no governmental safety net. We didn't have WIC, Medicaid, or Medicare. There was no Temporary Assistance for Needy Families or block grants for the indigent.

While there was no governmental system of aid to the down-and-out, there were those temple-goers whose pity and compassion would move them to give alms. Within their religious tradition, there was a concern for the poor. So, every day, I sat at one of the gates, where I would beg for alms. Though they saw me, no one invited me to go with them inside the temple. They just passed by me as they went in and as they went out. As people would enter or leave the temple, some would break a piece of change off for a brother.

Then one day, I see two men walking toward the temple. I would later learn that their names are Peter and John. They are a part of the group known as The People of the Way. They are Jesus-followers. They are the initial members of the church.

I'm outside the gate of the temple, the religious headquarters of Orthodox Judaism, where I received alms to assuage and accommodate my condition. Coming toward me are Peter and John, representatives of this new thing called the church of Jesus Christ. As I see them coming, I'm wondering what they will do. What are they about? What's their deal? What will be their response to me? Are they the same or are they different? If they are different, what is the point of their difference? What's the essence of it?

I'm aware that you, Reader, are seeking to more fully understand and appreciate the nature and calling of the church. God is calling you to be renewed and revived in your understanding of the church so that you more authentically can be the church—because you can't be what you don't get.

UNITY IN DIVERSITY

There are several things that I got about the church from my experience with Peter and John. One is, *the church thrives when it demonstrates unity in the midst of diversity.* Peter and John were together. John is the contemplative— quiet, spiritual, deep, the revelator, the one who gives us,

"In the beginning was the Word" (John 1:1). Peter, on the other hand, is the impulsive—loud, brash, crude, the one given to mood shifts, and who could cuss you and cut you. Two extremely different persons were together, paired by Jesus. They are a team. They reflect unity in the midst of diversity. That is what the church is meant to be.

Each was comfortable being who he is. John is John, and Peter is Peter. They could not be who they were meant to be trying to be the other. Jesus did not make them into the other because he knew that each had something unique that the kingdom needed. While this is so, the kingdom needed more than just them in their uniqueness; the kingdom needed them in their combined strength, in their collectiveness. Neither could be whom he needed to be without the other. The kingdom witness could not reach its fullest with them apart. They needed to be together.

There was no room for jealousy or pride. Each of them could have been moved by pride. Peter was the one who declared Jesus to be the Christ, the Son of the Living God. John was the beloved disciple, the one who leaned on Jesus' breast and to whom Jesus entrusted Mary, his earthly mother. Nevertheless, they are a team. They complement each other. They celebrate each other.

The church thrives when it demonstrates unity in the midst of diversity. God desires for us to appreciate and celebrate our uniqueness, our diversity, while at the same time recognizing and demonstrating our unity. There is a unique calling that God makes upon us as individuals and congregations, but there is also a collective call that God makes upon us as the body of Christ. It takes all of us working together to provide a complete witness to the glory of God. It takes all of us to take the gospel into all of the world.

So this day, I see these two completely different fellows walking together. I assume my usual posture of solicitation. They stop, and Peter says, "Look at us." Fasten your eyes on us. Pay attention. Check out our story. If you want a picture of the power of God, look on us.

Notice that he doesn't say, "Look at me." He says, "Look at us." In order for me to get the picture that is necessary for this work of God, looking at Peter or John individually would not be enough. I would need to see them in their collectivity rather than their individuality. When we look on the full body of Christ, we see a much more powerful story; we see a fuller picture of God's power.

EVANGELISTIC ILLUSTRATIONS

By inviting me to look at them, Peter was inviting me to behold an evangelistic illustration. I was looking at who Christ has made them to become. I was seeing what a tremendous work Christ had done in their lives.

The church dares to present evangelistic illustrations. Jesus seeks to use his followers as illustrations of his love and power. Before Peter and John proclaim one thing, they offer themselves as illustrations. They stand before me as signs and symbols of who Jesus is and what Jesus can do. By looking at them, I behold supernatural calm and courage that they did not have before they met Jesus. By looking at them, I see a unity of resolve and purpose that they did not possess before Jesus. By looking at them, I see a compassion and concern that came from Jesus. By looking at them, I receive an illustration that arrests my attention.

God seeks to do the same with you today. God seeks to use you as evangelistic illustrations. People should be invited to look at you and see something that points to who Christ is and what Christ is able to do. They should be able to see something about you that is Christ-developed, Christ-grown, Christlike. There should be something about your bearing, your demeanor, your persona, your aura, your walk, and your way that illustrates Christ without you having to say anything.

AN OFFER OF TRANSFORMATION

So I looked at them even more intently, expecting to receive something. Peter then says, "Silver and gold I do not have, but what I do have I give you: In the name of Jesus Christ of Nazareth, rise up and walk" (Acts 3:6 NKJV). Now, you need to know that Peter was neither broke nor penniless. People brought the funds and laid them at the apostles' feet. Peter had silver and some gold. The word for *have* in this instance refers to the basis of life; the basis of Peter's life was not silver and gold.

Peter was coming at me on a level that I had not expected. I had been using silver and gold as an accommodation to where my life was. I was expecting more accommodation from them. But I didn't need accommodation, I needed transformation. I needed a change. While I was looking for a hookup, Peter was calling me to rise up. He was calling for transformation.

The aim and offering of the church is not the accommodation of life, but the transformation of life. The church exists not to offer accommodation and maintenance of the status quo, *the church exists to offer transformation*. Ours is not an offer of silver and gold to make you feel better about a life of lameness. Ours is an offer of life transformation, it is of leaving lameness behind.

Herein is a rub. Because for many, the church has become a place where they are simply made better, sort of a religious improvement society. However, the call of the church is not to make better sinners or sinners better. The church's charge is to lead someone into a transformative experience with Jesus Christ that changes who they are. The church is called to be a transformative society with the goal of persons being conformed to the image of Christ. It is to lead people into ever deepening relationship with and likeness of Jesus. It is to offer transformation. Jesus said, "Very truly I tell you, no one can see the kingdom of God unless they are born again" (John 3:3). It is a call to transformation, to be dead to sin and alive to righteousness. "Therefore if anyone is in Christ, the new creation has come: The old has gone, the new is here!" (2 Corinthians 5:17).

Peter knew about transformation. Jesus met him when he was Simon bar Jonah. Upon seeing him, Jesus pronounced who he would become. Jesus announced the transformation that was to come. Jesus did not rest until that transformation came to pass.

THE RESURRECTION POWER OF JESUS

Mindful of that, Peter says, "In the name of Jesus Christ of Nazareth, rise up and walk." The transformation would not happen by my power; the power to rise up was tied to the person of Jesus Christ. The name of Jesus is associated with the power to get up and to walk. It is to rise to a newness of life and live within that newness.

The church is the body that proclaims the name of Jesus in resurrection power. Through Jesus, the power of resurrection is available. The capacity to get up, to rise above one's current condition, is made available through Jesus. To the lame man lowered from the ceiling by his friends, Jesus said, "Arise" (Mark 2:1-12 NKJV). To the man at the pool of Bethesda, Jesus said, "Rise . . . and walk" (John 5:8 NKJV). On at least three occasions, Jesus raised people from the dead. And most profoundly, after having been crucified on a cross on a Friday, God raised Jesus from the dead on the third day with all power in his hand. Because of this, we have a living hope through the resurrection of Jesus Christ from the dead.

To those who are down, who've been knocked down, there is the proclamation of resurrection in the name of Jesus. There is the proclamation that when we grow faint, weary, and fall, God is able to renew our strength and cause us to mount up on wings like an eagle, run and not get weary, walk and not faint (Isaiah 40:31 NKJV). He is the very power to mount up, to rise up, and to get up.

Peter told me, "In the name of Jesus Christ of Nazareth, rise up and walk" (Acts 3:6 NKJV). Then Peter took me by the right hand. While others had either left me, looked over me, or looked past me, Peter took me. Peter touched me. Peter established a connection with me. He established solidarity with me. It's when Peter took hold of me and lifted me up that strength came to my feet and ankles. It's when Peter helped me up that I was able to get up.

Some getting up, some rising up can't happen with mere proclamation. There also must be some reclamation, there must be some taking hold of. The church is the community that puts its hands toward what its mouth has spoken. With Peter having spoken about my rising up, Peter put his hands to work toward my rising up.

That is the call and charge to the church. People need more than proclamation, they need reclamation. They need the extension of hands into the concrete circumstances of their lives to help them rise up into what we have proclaimed.

The question to every believer is *What are you doing with your hands?* I know what you say out of your mouth, but are your hands actively engaged on what you say that you care about? Are you talking out of your mouth and expecting everybody else's hands to make it come to pass? Are you willing to extend your hands to help care for a child? Are you willing to extend your hands to help feed? Are you willing to extend your hands to repair what's been broken?

FELLOWSHIP IN JESUS

Peter extended his hands and power came. I began to get up—I stood up—I leaped up. I can't tell you how good that felt. I had been down for so long. Now, I was up. But I'm up with nowhere to go. What will I do with myself? I'm in a new posture. Will I go back to my old setting?

Peter and John invite me to go with them. I'd heard the psalms sung from a distance. I'd heard the prayers prayed from a distance. I'd heard the Scriptures read from a distance. I was always on the periphery, on the outside, but they invite me to join them. I get to go with them and heed the words of the psalmist, "Enter into his gates with thanksgiving, and into his courts with praise: be thankful unto him, and bless his name" (Psalm 100:4 KJV). I make my way with them. When I get there, I don't need a praise team. I bring my praise with me.

The church offers affirming and freeing fellowship. With Peter and John, I was affirmed in my worship and free to worship. As I worshiped, people began to look at me. I was vaguely familiar to them, but they couldn't believe what they were seeing. They were used to seeing me lying down, begging. Now, I was standing, leaping, and praising God. And I wasn't by myself—I had Peter and John. The closer that the people came to me, the tighter I held on to Peter and John. In the midst of the Law and Prophets being read and the Psalms being sung, I was praising the name of Jesus.

With Peter and John, I had company in the celebration of Jesus. I had to celebrate his name. It was in his name that I was standing whole. It was in his name that I had the power to walk. It was in his name that I rose up and walked. It was in his name that I left a life of begging. It was all in his name. Peter and John provided me with the fellowship that celebrates Jesus.

That is the church of the Lord Jesus Christ. We are the fellowship that celebrates his name. The name of Jesus is the only name under heaven given among men whereby we must be saved (Acts 4:12). The name of Jesus is highly exalted above every other name. At the name of Jesus, every knee must bow, of things in heaven, of things on earth, and of things under the earth, and every tongue must confess that he is Lord to the glory of God the Father (Philippians 2:9-11). Now I come to church to join with others who've come to celebrate Jesus who transforms us.

9

OFFERING A WORD FROM GOD

Now as the lame man who was healed held on to Peter and John, all the people ran together to them in the porch which is called Solomon's, greatly amazed. So when Peter saw it, he responded to the people: "Men of Israel, why do you marvel at this? Or why look so intently at us, as though by our own power or godliness we had made this man walk? The God of Abraham, Isaac, and Jacob, the God of our fathers, glorified His Servant Jesus, whom you delivered up and denied in the presence of Pilate, when he was determined to let Him go. But you denied the Holy One and the Just, and asked for a murderer to be granted to you, and killed the Prince of life, whom God raised from the dead, of which we are witnesses. And His name, through faith in His name, has made this man strong, whom you see and know. Yes, the faith which comes through Him has given him this perfect soundness in the presence of you all.

"Yet now, brethren, I know that you did it in ignorance, as did also your rulers. But those things which God foretold by the mouth of all His prophets, that the Christ would suffer, He has thus fulfilled. Repent therefore and be converted, that your sins may be blotted out, so that times of refreshing may come from the presence of the Lord, and that He may send Jesus Christ, who was preached to you before, whom heaven must receive until the times of restoration of all things, which God has spoken by the mouth of all His holy prophets since the world began. For Moses truly said to the fathers, 'The LORD your God will raise up for you a Prophet like me from your brethren. Him you shall hear in all things, whatever He says to you. And it shall be that every soul who will not hear that Prophet shall be utterly destroyed from among the people.' Yes, and all the prophets, from Samuel and those who follow, as many as have spoken, have also foretold these days. You are sons of the prophets, and of the covenant which God made with our fathers, saying to Abraham, 'And in your seed all the families of the earth shall be blessed.' To you first, God, having raised up His Servant Jesus, sent Him to bless you, in turning away every one of you from your iniquities." (Acts 3:11-26 NKJV).

With the undeniable change, unashamed identification, and uninhibited praise of the man who was lame from birth having arrested the attention of the worshippers at the temple, Peter senses an opportunity that he has not had within the confines of the temple. Prior to this episode, the temple was a place of tense feelings for the followers of

Jesus, because it was the seat from which the enemies of Jesus operated. The base of operations for the anti-Jesus movement was the temple where the Sanhedrin Council gathered under the leadership of the chief priest. While Peter and John were heading to the temple to pray, they were heading there desirous of being inconspicuous. But they came across the man who was lame and introduced him to the transforming power of Jesus Christ. The man's response to their having done so captures the attention of the people and places all eyes on them.

When Peter sees that, he is faced with an interpretive decision. How does he see them? One translation reads, "When Peter saw he had a congregation . . ." (Acts 3:12 *The Message*). He sees them as an audience. Seeing that, he opens his mouth and begins to address the crowd. Having gained the attention of the crowd, he has a word for them to hear.

A WORD FOR OTHERS

The church of Jesus Christ is the group of people who understand that, having gained the attention of people around them, they have a word that those people need to hear. With God having drawn attention to them by what God did for them, they had the opportunity to speak a word on behalf of God.

God's desire, for we who make up the church, is to recognize that the attention that people pay to us is created by him and for his purposes. We must rightly interpret the attention that people pay to us.

Some of us may know what it is for God to work within our life and have people look at us in amazement. They didn't expect us to get as far as we've gotten. They didn't expect us to withstand what we've withstood. They didn't expect us to come back from the disappointment the way that we have. They didn't expect us to be put back together. It amazes them. It astonishes them. They're amazed that we're standing. They're amazed that we're thriving. They're amazed that we're prospering. They're amazed that we're sober. They're amazed that we're working. They're amazed that we're not bitter; that we're smiling; that we're worshiping.

God wants us to know that as they stare at us, as they look amazed at us, as they scratch their heads trying to figure us out, it's never by us or for us.

The work that he does for us, through us, or in us that catches their attention and directs their focus toward us is so that we are able to say something on behalf of him. Whatever influence or sway that we possess is never simply by us or for us. It is ultimately by God and for God.

With people's curiosity, fascination, or wonder about us, about our achievement, about our success, about our recovery, about our consistency, about our pleasant demeanor, we have a chance to share a word about God that they need to hear.

God gives us an audience, a congregation for us to share a word about him. Our family is a congregation. Our friends are a congregation. Our coworkers and neighbors are congregations.

A WORD THAT BRINGS GOD GLORY

Seeing that all eyes were on them, Peter steps up with a word for them to hear. He begins by saying, "Fellow Israelites, why does this surprise you? Why do you stare at us as if by our own power or godliness we had made this man walk? The God of Abraham, Isaac and Jacob, the God of our fathers, has glorified his servant Jesus. You handed him over to be killed, and you disowned him before Pilate, though he had decided to let him go" (Acts 3:12-13). With the people staring at them, Peter is quick to redirect their attention. He acknowledges that what they see in the lame man now standing has absolutely nothing to do with them, but everything to do with God. Recognizing the propensity of people to misapply the credit, Peter lets them know that the credit belongs to God. It was God. In God's work, God brought glory to the name of Jesus.

The church offers a word that directs glory to God. Whenever people witness the work of God within our life and are impacted by the results of that work, there is the call to glorify God. As the crowd was in Peter and John's time, such is the case now. People are prone to misapply the credit. They will attribute it to so many other things. They will talk about their family background, their social network, their educational pedigree, and so on. But we must know that it's not about any of that—it's about God.

In those cases, the call of the people of God is to be found offering a word that glorifies God rather than promoting the self. It's being found answering the questions: How did you make it? *God.* How did you handle it? *God.* How did you bear it? *God.* How did you overcome it? *God.* How did you see that? *God.* How did you learn it? *God.* How did you attain it? *God.* How have you kept it? *God.*

As the people stand in astonishment looking at Peter, John, and the man who was lame, Peter knows that there is more to what they see. The man whom they see now standing is standing by his faith in the name of Jesus. By healing the man, God brought honor to the name of Jesus.

To fully appreciate this, you must remember that they are in the temple in Jerusalem. This was the very place where Jesus was mistried, and handed over to Pilate to be crucified. And it is in this very place that God honors the name of Jesus by healing the man through faith in the name of Jesus. Peter makes this plain with the words,

> The God of Abraham, Isaac, and Jacob, the God of our fathers, glorified His Servant Jesus, whom you delivered up and denied in the presence of Pilate, when he was determined to let Him go. But you denied the Holy One and the Just, and asked for a murderer to be granted to you, and killed the Prince of life, whom God

raised from the dead, of which we are witnesses. And His name, through faith in His name, has made this man strong, whom you see and know. Yes, the faith which comes through Him has given him this perfect soundness in the presence of you all. "Yet now, brethren, I know that you did it in ignorance, as did also your rulers. But those things which God foretold by the mouth of all His prophets, that the Christ would suffer, He has thus fulfilled." (Acts 3:13-18 NKJV)

A WORD THAT EXPLAINS THE WORKING OF GOD

Even though the people were religious, they were clueless to the working of God in Jesus. They were ignorant and blind to God's work. God desired to clue them in to how he worked within what they did to Jesus: They rejected Jesus. They chose a murderer named Barabbas over Jesus. They crucified Jesus. But God took all of it to fulfill what God had declared through the prophets centuries before. Though they crucified, Jesus, God raised Jesus to life.

With the people in awe of the man whom they see now walking and leaping, Peter connects the dots to what God did for him with what God has done for and through Jesus. Blessed with the gift of historical memory, Peter is able to explain the way and working of God.

The church not only seeks to offer a word that directs glory to God, but also a word that clarifies and explains the working of God. When people see the result of God working in our life, there is a call for us to explain to them what it is really about and what it really means. People are astonished by the glory that they see, but we must see God's call to tell them the story that's behind the glory.

Believers must be found telling how God was present within the disjointed, the disconnected, the dysfunctional, the disappointing, and the distressing events and episodes of our lives and working them together for the good. We must be found talking about how our thoughts were not God's thoughts and our ways were not God's ways, how God may not have come when we wanted him, but he was on time when he came.

We must be heard speaking the word that explains the faithfulness of God is not just seen in the immediate and momentary. The faithfulness of God is also seen in the delayed and in the longer term. It's seen in the midst of even what seems to be a contradiction. To many, Calvary appeared to be a contradiction of Jesus, the ultimate refutation of Jesus' claims. But God was using what looked like a contradiction and refutation to further God's fulfillment and vindication.

To a generation that judges everything by the speed and ease by which things happen and come their way, there is a need for the ways of God to be clarified and explained, that God isn't always in the swift and the easy. God is often in the difficult and slow. God isn't limited to the loud and showy. God is often in the silent and obscured.

There are those who know that so much more of life is spent where the lines are not always clearly seen and the name of God may not even be on the page. But they've discovered that he's in the story even when he isn't on the page. And where they don't see the line between the dots, he is the line. He's there filling the gaps. They know that God is the line; God is filling the gaps in between.

A WORD THAT INVITES RELATIONSHIP

Having directed glory to God and having clarified and explained the working of God to the people, Peter has them where he wants them. Peter continues,

> Repent therefore and be converted, that your sins may be blotted out, so that times of refreshing may come from the presence of the Lord, and that He may send Jesus Christ, who was preached to you before, whom heaven must receive until the times of restoration of all things, which God has spoken by the mouth of all His holy prophets since the world began. (Acts 3:19-21 NKJV)

With the people looking in astonishment, Peter understands that their real need is not the mere satisfaction of their curiosity. Their real need is a relationship with God that is real and personal. They had ritual and even religion. But they had no relationship with God. Therefore, Peter calls them to repent and to turn to God. There is a cleansing from sin that they need and God wants to provide. There is refreshment, renewal, and revival that they can experience through the presence of the Lord in their lives.

If they thought that the healing of the lame man was something, they can have even more. They can have their sins forgiven, their souls refreshed, their minds renewed, and their lives changed. All that they need to do is repent and turn to God.

As the church, we are not only called to give a word that directs people to glorify God, and a word that clarifies and explains the workings of God, but also a word that invites people to a relationship with God. Our speech must never be satisfied with clarification or glorification—there must be invitation. From us a curious and needy world must receive an invitation. From us must come the words: If you're looking for real life, I've got something for you. If you're looking for something genuine and authentic, I've got something for you. Are you looking for something fresh? I've got something for you. Are you looking for something lasting? I've got something for you. Are you looking for real joy? I've got something for you. Are you looking for inner peace of mind and spirit? I've got something for you. Are you tired of where you are and how you are? I've got something for you. Do you want something more for your life and to your life? I have something for you.

We don't just have something for others. We have some *one* for others. We want to invite others to meet him. We met him through an invitation. We heard him say, "Come to Me, all you who labor and are heavy laden, and I will give you rest. Take My yoke upon you and learn from Me, for I am gentle and lowly in heart" (Matthew 11:28-29 NKJV). We received an invitation from a hill called Calvary. As Jesus was hung high and stretched wide, he was inviting us. As he was shedding his blood for the taking away of our sins, he was inviting us. As he died there on the cross, he was inviting us. As God raised him from the dead on the third day, he was inviting us.

"I heard the voice of Jesus say come unto Me and rest. Lay down thy weary one lay down thy head upon My breast. I came to Jesus as I was weary, worn, and sad. I found in Him a resting place, He has made me glad."[1] I accepted his invitation. He's changed my life. He's the best thing that ever happened to me. I invite you to meet him. I invite you to meet Jesus, the Bread of Life, the Light of the World, the Good Shepherd, the Door, the Resurrection and the Life, the Way, the Truth, and the Life, the True Vine, the Alpha and Omega, the Beginning and the Ending, the First and the Last, the One who lives, who was dead, and who is alive forevermore and who possesses the keys to death and hell.

He's able to refresh you. He's able to renew you. He's able to revive you.

10

EVIDENT BOLDNESS

Now as they spoke to the people, the priests, the captain of the temple, and the Sadducees came upon them, being greatly disturbed that they taught the people and preached in Jesus the resurrection from the dead. And they laid hands on them, and put them in custody until the next day, for it was already evening. However, many of those who heard the word believed; and the number of the men came to be about five thousand.

And it came to pass, on the next day, that their rulers, elders, and scribes, as well as Annas the high priest, Caiaphas, John, and Alexander, and as many as were of the family of the high priest, were gathered together at Jerusalem. And when they had set them in the midst, they asked, "By what power or by what name have you done this?"

Then Peter, filled with the Holy Spirit, said to them, "Rulers of the people and elders of Israel: If we this day are judged for a good deed done to a helpless man, by what means he has been made well, let it be known to you all, and to all the people of Israel, that by the name of Jesus Christ of Nazareth, whom you crucified, whom God raised from the dead, by Him this man stands here before you whole. This is the 'stone which was rejected by you builders, which has become the chief cornerstone.' Nor is there salvation in any other, for there is no other name under heaven given among men by which we must be saved."

Now when they saw the boldness of Peter and John, and perceived that they were uneducated and untrained men, they marveled. And they realized that they had been with Jesus. And seeing the man who had been healed standing with them, they could say nothing against it. But when they had commanded them to go aside out of the council, they conferred among themselves, saying, "What shall we do to these men? For, indeed, that a notable miracle has been done through them is evident to all who dwell in Jerusalem, and we cannot deny it. But so that it spreads no further among the people, let us severely threaten them, that from now on they speak to no man in this name."

So they called them and commanded them not to speak at all nor teach in the name of Jesus. But Peter and John answered and said to them, "Whether it is right in the sight of God to listen to you more than to God, you judge. For we cannot but speak the things which we

> have seen and heard." So when they had further
> threatened them, they let them go, finding no way of
> punishing them, because of the people, since they all
> glorified God for what had been done. For the man
> was over forty years old on whom this miracle of
> healing had been performed. (Acts 4:1-22 NKJV)

With their arrest and jailing, Peter and John experience the first instance of the persecution of the church. The next day, as they stand before the Sanhedrin to give an account for the hope that they have, an impression is made on those who oppose them. Luke observes that those who examined them knew that they had been with Jesus. While the religious leaders may have disagreed with Peter and John and while they may have denied the claims of Jesus themselves, they couldn't deny that Peter and John had been with Jesus. They knew that they spent time with Jesus and that Jesus spent time with them.

There is a message from this that we are to get: *The church is the community whose lifestyle gives evidence to having been with Jesus.* There should be something about the people who name the name of Jesus that causes people who observe us to know that we've been with the Lord. They should be able to conclude that the relationship is more than just a casual association and a mere acquaintance. They should be able to consider our manner of life and conclude that we've been with Jesus.

BOLDNESS FROM BEING WITH JESUS

They noticed the boldness of Peter and John and concluded that they had been with Jesus. Peter and John possessed a confidence and assurance. There was no sense of intimidation upon them. There was no evidence of uncertainty about them and the position that they took. They did not backpedal. They stood with an air of audacity. Though they stood in the midst of an anti-Jesus environment, they were assertive in their position.

The church is the community whose boldness gives evidence to having been with Jesus. There is a certain level of boldness that only Jesus can give. There is an assurance that transcends our surroundings and a daring that defies that to which a natural person would succumb. It is a sense that what we believe is right and worth standing for, regardless of the case. When we've spent time with Christ and he's spent time with us, he gives a calm courage that allows us to state our case and not flinch, to be still while others are running and hiding. A life in Christ produces a boldness to speak truth where and when people don't want to hear it, to call a spade a spade, to call wrong, wrong; right, right; truth, truth; and injustice, injustice. Peter and John stood without fear of the consequences. As Peter and John stood before the very enemies of Jesus, the enemies knew that they had been with Jesus because they had seen that very same boldness in Jesus. Countless times, they witnessed Jesus' courage in their presence.

Jesus never flinched before them. He stood with certainty and confidence.

WISDOM AND KNOWLEDGE

It is with that very same confidence that Peter and John stood before these leaders. But it was more than just their boldness. It was also their wisdom and knowledge. Peter and John displayed a level of competence that went beyond their formal education. As they stood in the temple, they were not just in the religious center of Jewish life, they were also in the educational center of Jewish life. It was in the temple where the great Jewish scholars taught. Neither Peter nor John are on record as having attended or audited any class taught by the religious scholars. They were unlearned Galileans, whose speech was Aramaic, not proper Hebrew. Yet, the content of their speech displayed a level of depth and sophistication that exceeded all expectations of them. What they lacked in rabbinical credit hours, God had more than supplied through their time with Jesus and the illumination of the Holy Spirit.

We give evidence of our having been with Jesus through the wisdom and knowledge that we display. God has a way of working with and through us that exceeds the parameters of what is expected of us and from us. From our autobiography and from our resumé, some things just aren't expected. Yet, God has a way of enabling us to be and to do the unexpected.

There Peter and John were in the presence of the learned, the PhDs, the DMins. They had no D, but they were able to speak the gospel message with clarity and conviction. They remembered the promise that Jesus made to them in Luke: "When they drag you into their meeting places, or into police courts and before judges, don't worry about defending yourselves—what you'll say and how you'll say it. The right words will be there. The Holy Spirit will give you the right words when the time comes" (Luke 12:11-12 *The Message*). The Lord fulfilled that word to them. The Holy Spirit gave them the right words at the right time.

When we've been with Jesus, he's able to do the same thing for us. Someone reading this knows that they didn't have a clue what they were going to say when they went into the interview, but when they arrived, he gave the right words at the right time. They didn't know what they were going to say when applying for the loan, but God gave them the right words at the right time. No one had a clue how to resolve the matter at work, but the Lord gave them the understanding and the words to say. They'd been there the least amount of time; they didn't have the pedigree that others had. But they did have Jesus. They did spend time with Jesus. Jesus gave just what they needed. He gave what they needed to see, to say, to know; what they needed to do, where they needed to go, who they needed to take.

When people see us in that way, they may not be able to put their finger exactly on what they're seeing, so they say things like, "You're an old soul . . . You've been here before . . ." It's just that we've spent time with Someone who's from everlasting to everlasting. We spend time with the One who sees the end from the beginning and the beginning to the end. When we spend time with him, he's able to download some stuff into us that is not of this world or of this time. It comes from him.

WORKS THAT LOOK LIKE JESUS

The Sanhedrin observes the boldness and wisdom and knowledge of Peter and John. They discern that what they see had to come from someone other than them. This had to be Jesus. But there was something else that led them to this conclusion. As they looked at Peter, John, and the healed lame man, they could not deny that the man who was lame from birth was now standing, walking, leaping, and praising God. They could not deny the fact that Peter and John had been used by God. The work of Peter and John spoke for itself.

Not only do we give evidence that we've spent time with Jesus through our boldness, and our wisdom and knowledge, but we also give evidence of having spent time with Jesus through our works.

The church gives evidence of having been with Jesus by its works. When we've spent time with Jesus, the actions that Jesus promotes will speak for themselves. We don't have to walk around with a big Jesus T-shirt or Jesus cape for people to know that we've been with Jesus. The work will speak for itself. When we let the light that he develops in us shine through us so that people see our good works, they'll recognize God and glorify him. When our time with Jesus prompts acts of kindness to flow from us, the kindness speaks for itself. When our time with Jesus sensitizes us to the type of conversations that we do and don't participate in, our refusal to gossip will speak for itself. That's why saints of old sang, "May the works I've done speak for me . . . May the life I live, speak for me . . ."

As the Sanhedrin looked at the healed man standing, they begrudgingly had to admit, "That looks like Jesus." They may not have liked Jesus, but he did make the lame to walk. That looks like Jesus.

A believer should act in such a way that even those who don't like Jesus have to admit that we've been with Jesus because our actions look like his actions. Our bringing peace to troubled situations looks like his calming the winds and the waves. Our feeding the hungry looks like his feeding the multitudes. Our acts of compassion toward people on the margins, our serving those affected by HIV, looks like his work with those on the margins, those believed to be untouchable. When they see us working to help disrupt the modern-day sex trade, they see his working to set the captive free. When they see us spending time to teach kids, to mentor kids, they see his working with the children, using children as object lessons of humility and trust. When they see us working to dismantle racial, ethnic, and gender disparity, they see Jesus destroying those barriers as he engaged the woman of Samaria at the well.

The Sanhedrin saw what Peter and John did and said, "That looks like Jesus." God is calling for his church to live and serve so that a watching world might be able to say: *That looks like Jesus.* They serve like Jesus. They console like Jesus. They bring peace like Jesus. They usher in healing like Jesus. They encourage like Jesus. They seek the lost like Jesus. They welcome the sinner like Jesus. They embrace the backslider like Jesus. They cover the vulnerable like Jesus

STEADFAST DETERMINATION

I must warn you that when you live such that people see that you've been with Jesus and that Jesus has been with you, some will view you to be a threat. As such, they will try to nullify you. They tried that with Peter and John. They sought to silence them. They brought them back and tied the condition of their release to no longer preaching or teaching in Jesus' name. They tried to create some mental and emotional distance between them and Jesus.

The same is true for us. When the enemy sees that our being with Jesus is a threat to his continued sway and influence around us, he will do what he can to create some distance between us and Jesus. He will raise covert and overt challenges to get us to deny or to absent ourselves from further involvement with Jesus.

It's in those moments that our time with Jesus will reveal another aspect of his character. It will reveal steadfast determination. Peter and John reject the offer. If it means staying in jail, so be it; they are determined to stay with Jesus.

The church is the community whose determination gives evidence to having spent time with Jesus. The steadfast commitment of followers of Jesus gives evidence of having spent time with Jesus.

As Peter and John stood unwavering in their commitment to Jesus, the Sanhedrin had seen that before. They saw it on the night of Jesus' trial. Nothing that they did broke Jesus' determination. They saw it with Jesus before Pilate: There was nothing that Pilate offered or that the soldiers did that broke Jesus' determination. The being spat upon, the being beaten, the placing of the crown of thorns on his head, the offering of release if he'd just say something to defend himself—nothing broke his determination. Neither the weight of the cross, the pain of the nails, the pulling down of gravity, the taunts from the crowd, the aches of his body, nor the darkness felt by his soul broke his determination. He remained determined. For the joy that was set before him, he endured the cross and despised the shame until his very last breath. He died determined. Early Sunday morning, God vindicated his determination by raising him up with all power in his hands.

Not only does the Sanhedrin, looking at Peter and John, say to themselves, "We've seen that determination before," but also God the Father says, "I've seen that before." God works in such a way that the Sanhedrin have to let them go.

When our life with Jesus empowers us to live a life that allows God to see the determination of his Son, God the Father will respond in power. God will fight on our behalf. God will move on our behalf. God will. I want the Father to see Jesus' determination in me.

11

LIVING IN THE TENSION

The next day the rulers, the elders and the teachers of the law met in Jerusalem. Annas the high priest was there, and so were Caiaphas, John, Alexander and others of the high priest's family. They had Peter and John brought before them and began to question them: "By what power or what name did you do this?"

Then Peter, filled with the Holy Spirit, said to them: "Rulers and elders of the people! If we are being called to account today for an act of kindness shown to a man who was lame and are being asked how he was healed, then know this, you and all the people of Israel: It is by the name of Jesus Christ of Nazareth, whom you crucified but whom God raised from the dead, that this man stands before you healed. Jesus is

"'the stone you builders rejected,
    which has become the cornerstone.'

Salvation is found in no one else, for there is no other name under heaven given to mankind by which we must be saved."

When they saw the courage of Peter and John and realized that they were unschooled, ordinary men, they were astonished and they took note that these men had been with Jesus. But since they could see the man who had been healed standing there with them, there was nothing they could say. So they ordered them to withdraw from the Sanhedrin and then conferred together. "What are we going to do with these men?" they asked. "Everyone living in Jerusalem knows they have performed a notable sign, and we cannot deny it. But to stop this thing from spreading any further among the people, we must warn them to speak no longer to anyone in this name."

Then they called them in again and commanded them not to speak or teach at all in the name of Jesus. But Peter and John replied, "Which is right in God's eyes: to listen to you, or to him? You be the judges! As for us, we cannot help speaking about what we have seen and heard."

After further threats they let them go. They could not decide how to punish them, because all the people were praising God for what had happened. For the man who was miraculously healed was over forty years old. (Acts 4:5-22)

Seeing the boldness, wisdom and knowledge, impactful work, and steadfast commitment and determination of

Peter and John, the Sanhedrin conclude that Peter and John must have been with Jesus.

As they look at the man, healed from a forty-year illness that had relegated him to life on the periphery, resigned to monetizing his dependency through begging, they do not share the jubilation of the crowd that gathered at Solomon's Porch. You would think that seeing a man who had been flat on his back and begging be transformed into one who is standing, walking, worshiping, and taking charge of his life is an occasion of joy and celebration. So powerful an experience was it for some, that they came to faith in Jesus on that very day. Luke tells us that many who heard the word believed, bringing the number of men who believed to that of five thousand. If you factor the number of female believers into the equation, the church is now between seventy-five hundred to ten thousand believers.

This presents a problem for the Sanhedrin, who see themselves as guardians of the tradition of the Law and the Prophets, and who believe Jesus and his followers to be heretical. They cannot argue the man's healing, it speaks for itself. Some things that the Lord does just speak for themselves. We don't have to say anything; what is seen says it all. When Jesus told a blind man whose sight was restored not to tell anybody, the man didn't have to say anything. Just his walking by himself, not needing anybody to show him and not needing a stick to warn him, said everything. When the townspeople from Gadara saw a man that had been possessed by a legion of demons that caused him to harass the people, commit self-mutilation, and run around naked, now seated, clothed, and in his right mind, the man didn't have to say anything; what they saw said everything. Somebody reading this knows that there are some works of the Lord in their life where they don't have to say a word. What people see says it all.

The man standing, leaping, and worshiping says it all. While they cannot deny the healing, they cannot allow attributing the healing to the person of Jesus. They thought that they, in effect, had handled the matter with Jesus' crucifixion. They saw him breathe his last breath, give up his spirit, and be buried in a tomb covered by a stone and guarded by soldiers. Then Sunday came with the fanciful story that angels appeared, rolled away the stone, and a resurrected Jesus left the tomb to later declare that all power in heaven and earth had been given unto him. It seemed odd to the Sanhedrin that this resurrected Jesus was only seen by his followers. If he was truly alive, why not appear to any of them? Notwithstanding, people were believing it and now the strongest piece of evidence stood before them in this man who was lame standing, walking, leaping, praising God and saying, "Only Jesus did it." That had to stop.

After having sent Peter and John out of the hearing room so that they could confer over the matter, the Sanhedrin call them back in and command them not to speak or teach in the name of Jesus.

This is not the local justice of the peace issuing the command. This is what is tantamount to the Jewish Supreme Court speaking with the force of law. Barely a few months old, the church of Jesus Christ experiences its first dose of persecution.

THE TENSION OF COMMITMENT

The church is the fellowship whose original and continual existence is within the tension created by a commitment to Jesus.

Consider the flow of Peter and John's appearance before the Sanhedrin. The only question that the Sanhedrin ask them is "By what power or what name did you do this?" (v. 7). To which Peter, filled with the Spirit responds, "Rulers and elders of the people! If we are being called to account today for an act of kindness shown to a man who was lame and are being asked how he was healed, then know this, you and all the people of Israel: It is by the name of Jesus Christ of Nazareth, whom you crucified but whom God raised from the dead, that this man stands before you healed" (vv. 8-10). Notice then, the particulars of the command. They are not commanded against healing. They are commanded to no longer speak or teach in the name of Jesus. For the Sanhedrin, the problem is not with the good works. The problem is with the One through whom the work is done and whose name is connected to the work. The world has no problem with good works. It has no problem with activity that it believes to be relevant to it.

Feed the hungry. Clothe the naked. Shelter the homeless. Heal the sick. Liberate the captive. All is fine by itself. Just don't attribute it to or present it as being done for the sake of, under the power of, or for the glory of Jesus.

The church is the community whose commitment to Christ produces tension. The Christian faith does not promise tension-free living. It assumes the presence of tension. In Matthew 16, Jesus asks the disciples two questions; "Who do people say the Son of Man is?" and "Who do you say I am?" (vv. 13, 15). To the second question, Simon Peter answered, "You are the Messiah, the Son of the living God" (v. 16). Jesus assured Simon that his answer was the result of divine revelation and that it is the central truth upon which the church is built. He also warned the disciples against the persecution that would come due to their allegiance to him and the temptations that would come to deny him. Consider the words of Jesus: "Blessed are you when people insult you, persecute you and falsely say all kinds of evil against you because of me" (Matthew 5:11); and

> But before all this, they will seize you and persecute you. They will hand you over to synagogues and put you in prison, and you will be brought before kings and governors, and all on account of my name. And so you will bear testimony to me. But make up your mind not to worry beforehand how you will defend yourselves. For I will give you words and wisdom that

none of your adversaries will be able to resist or contradict. You will be betrayed even by parents, brothers and sisters, relatives and friends, and they will put some of you to death. Everyone will hate you because of me. (Luke 21:12-17)

Commitment to Christ, identification with Christ, and the proclamation of Christ produces tension.

As Peter and John stand before what is tantamount to the Supreme Court of the Jews, they are commanded to no longer speak or teach in the name of Jesus. Continue their acts of charity, just don't mention Jesus. They can even preach and teach from Adam to John the Baptist. Just don't lift the name of Jesus.

The casual observer might wonder what's the problem. Is the name of Jesus that important? Those who innocently ask the question do so not realizing that to exclude Christ from the speech of the Christian is to ask the Christian to fundamentally deny the core of his or her religious identity. While the essence of other faiths may be devotion to a creed, the adherence to a code, the practice of a discipline, or the pursuit of a path, the Christian faith is built upon a devotion to a person. To deny the centrality and uniqueness of the person of Jesus Christ is to deny the Christian faith itself.

The church's infancy is within the context of the tension that commitment to Christ produces. The church's context continues to be the tension that commitment to Christ produces. According to Pew Research, Christians are the most persecuted group in the world.[1] Open Doors reports that 5,898 Christians were killed for their beliefs worldwide in 2021. They estimate that nearly 360 million Christians faced persecution and discrimination for practicing their faith.[2] In many places on earth, being a Christian is the most dangerous thing that a person can be.

While the degree and manifestation of the tension may vary, a commitment to Christ produces tension. We who live in the United States currently may not face the threat of loss of life due to identification with Jesus; there is tension nonetheless. Increasingly, there is marginalization of the name of Jesus. There is the pressure to not mention his name in public prayers. There is the pressure to downplay his uniqueness. There is the greater tendency to portray him in ways that are inconsistent with the Scriptures. On college and university campuses there is pressure to deny official standing to Christian organizations who continue to require a commitment to Christ for those who would serve as officers in leadership.

THE TENSION THROUGH THE AGES

The wonder of the church is not simply the fact that its beginning members were an unlikely crew of people who didn't know what they were getting into, but also the fact that the likelihood of the church surviving the opposition to it and persecution of it was slim-to-none. Beginning as a marginalized and persecuted subsect of Judaism that would later suffer persecution under the most dominant power in the world (the Roman Empire, which stretched from England to Africa and from Syria to Spain), bets on the church's survival would not have been great. In fact, many bet against its survival. The Roman Emperor Diocletian, whose reign between AD 284–305 characterized one of the most brutal periods of Christian persecution by Rome, sent the church into hiding in caves and worshiping in catacombs. He was so confident that he had made an end of the church that he minted a coin with this motto on it: "The Christian religion is destroyed and the worship of the Roman gods is restored."

Yet the fact that Christians gather some two thousand years since first being told to no longer speak or teach in Jesus' name, bears witness that neither the socioreligious pressure of the Sanhedrin nor the imperial power of Rome were able to shatter the commitment of the faithful followers of Jesus. Diocletian is dead and gone. The names of the Roman gods Jupiter, Juno, Neptune, Minerva, Mars, Venus, Apollo, Diana, Vulcan, Vesta, Mercury, and Ceres have long faded from public adoration and reverence. But the name of Jesus is still lifted from the darkened halls of the catacombs of Rome to the sunlit plaza of St. Peter's Square.

Please understand: It is no small or light thing to be a recipient of the gospel of Jesus Christ. It is to have received a life-transforming message that came not just at the cost of the life, death, and resurrection of Jesus, but also at the cost of the lives and livelihoods of thousands upon thousands of saints throughout the ages who endured torture, mocking, stoning, chains, being sawed in two, fed to lions, burned at the stake, driven to hiding out in the wilderness, in dens, and in caves (Hebrews 11:36-38). It is to also inherit the tension that a commitment to Christ produces.

THE INTEGRITY OF THEIR EXPERIENCE

There Peter and John are, standing before the supreme tribunal of Jewish Law, the Sanhedrin, being commanded not to speak or teach in the name of Jesus. Peter and John respond, "Which is right in God's eyes: to listen to you, or to him? You be the judges! As for us, we cannot help speaking about what we have seen and heard" (Acts 4:19-20). Against the pressure to diminish and even deny their identification and commitment to Christ, Peter and John assert the integrity of their experience with Christ. To deny Christ, to downplay Christ, to discount Christ, to dismiss talk of Christ, would be to deny the integrity of their experience with Christ. They say, "We cannot but speak of the things that we've seen and heard."

We've seen some things and we've heard some things. We are eyewitnesses to some things. Therefore, we can't help but speak what we've witnessed. We can't help but speak what we've seen and heard. We can't speak what we haven't seen or heard. We speak what we've seen and what we've heard. We talk about Jesus because we can't help but talk about him. He is what we speak because he is whom we've seen and heard. What we've seen and heard gives us something to talk about.

If we had not met Jesus, we wouldn't have anything specific to talk about—all that we could be is general. But since we met him, saw him, and heard him, we can't help but be specific and speak and teach in his name. Peter and John assert the integrity of their experience with Jesus. John would later write:

> That which was from the beginning, which we have heard, which we have seen with our eyes, which we have looked at and our hands have touched—this we proclaim concerning the Word of life. The life appeared; we have seen it and testify to it, and we proclaim to you the eternal life, which was with the Father and has appeared to us. We proclaim to you what we have seen and heard, so that you also may have fellowship with us. And our fellowship is with the Father and with his Son, Jesus Christ. (1 John 1:1-3)

And Peter would later write:

> For we were not making up clever stories when we told you about the powerful coming of our Lord Jesus Christ. We saw his majestic splendor with our own eyes when he received honor and glory from God the Father. The voice from the majestic glory of God said

to him, "This is my dearly loved Son, who brings me great joy." We ourselves heard that voice from heaven when we were with him on the holy mountain. (2 Peter 1:16-18 NLT)

They assert the integrity of their experience. They'd seen and heard Jesus. They'd seen Jesus turn water into wine. They'd seen Jesus heal a nobleman's son from a distance. They'd seen Jesus heal a chronically lame man at the pool. They'd seen Jesus feed five thousand men, not counting women and children, with two fish and five loaves of bread. They'd seen Jesus walk on the water and calm the storm. They'd seen Jesus give sight to a man who was blind from birth. They'd seen Jesus raise Jairus's daughter, the widow of Nain's son, and Lazarus from the dead. They'd seen too much and they'd heard too much.

At their first meeting, Peter, then known as Simon, heard Jesus tell him, "You are Simon son of John. You will be called Cephas" (John 1:42). After spending a night of fishing and catching nothing, Peter and John heard Jesus tell them to launch out into the deep for a catch. In obedience to his word, they did so and caught more than their boat could hold. They heard him tell the winds and the waves "Quiet! Be still!" and they obeyed his voice (Mark 4:39). They heard him tell the demons called Legion to come out of the man and they obeyed his voice and departed (Mark 5:1-20). They heard him tell a man who was lowered from the rooftop to rise, take up his bed, and walk, and the man obeyed his voice (Mark 2:1-5). They heard him stop a mob intent on stoning a woman who had been caught in adultery with the words, "Let any one of you who is without sin be the first to throw a stone at her" (John 8:7).

Before he died, they heard him talk about his death and his resurrection. He did just what he said. They heard him say,

> Go into all the world and preach the gospel to all creation. Whoever believes and is baptized will be saved, but whoever does not believe will be condemned. And these signs will accompany those who believe: In my name they will drive out demons; they will speak in new tongues; they will pick up snakes with their hands; and when they drink deadly poison, it will not hurt them at all; they will place their hands on sick people, and they will get well. (Mark 16:15-18)

Before ascending into heaven, they'd heard him say, "You will be my witnesses in Jerusalem, and in all Judea and Samaria, and to the ends of the earth" (Acts 1:8).

THE INTEGRITY OF OUR EXPERIENCE

They asserted the integrity of their experience. *The church is the body that confronts the tension by asserting the integrity of its experience with Christ.* As believers in Christ, we can't help but speak what we've seen and heard. Ours is not a story of imagined things. It is a story of what we've seen and what we've heard.

> For God so loved the world that he gave his one and only Son, that whoever believes in him shall not perish but have eternal life. (John 3:16)

> Whoever hears my word and believes him who sent me has eternal life and will not be judged but has crossed over from death to life. (John 5:24)

> Seek first his kingdom and his righteousness, and all these things will be given to you as well. (Matthew 6:33)

> Ask and it will be given to you; seek and you will find; knock and the door will be opened to you. (Matthew 7:7)

> Do not let your hearts be troubled. You believe in God; believe also in me. My Father's house has many rooms; if that were not so, would I have told you that I am going there to prepare a place for you? And if I go and prepare a place for you, I will come back and take you to be with me that you also may be where I am. (John 14:1-3)

> I have told you these things, so that in me you may have peace. In this world you will have trouble. But take heart! I have overcome the world. (John 16:33)

We assert the integrity of our experience.

Have you seen the change that Jesus has made in your life? You saw where you were before you met him. You saw where you were headed before you met him. You saw what you were powerless against before you met him. Have you seen what you couldn't overcome before you met him? Have you seen the change that he's made in your life? Someone reading this can say, "I've seen the transformation. I've seen the shifts. I've seen the deliverance. I've seen the healing. I've seen the breakthroughs. I haven't just seen it in my life, but I've seen it in the lives of others. I've seen it in the lives of my parents. I've seen it in the lives of my children. I've seen it in the lives of friends and prayer partners."

We've seen him take the desire for the drugs away. We've seen him deliver from addiction. We've seen him transform lifestyles and sexual behavior. We've seen him restore joy and renew peace. We've seen him lift burdens. We've seen him fight battles. If we hadn't seen it, we couldn't talk about it. But since we've seen it, we can't help but talk about it.

COMPELLED BY CHRIST'S LOVE

In the face of the socioreligious structure of their day, Peter and John asserted the integrity of their experience. But also they could not give in to the tension because they were compelled by his love for them. The ultimate aim of the tension is to create distance in their relationship with Jesus. The belief is that the fear of consequences to their commitment to Christ is greater than their love for Christ. Peter and John demonstrate that the compulsion of Christ's love is greater than the fear of the Sanhedrin's threats. The night before he died, they saw his love for them unto the very end. They saw him give his life as a ransom for us all. John saw him at the cross, dying for us. They both saw the empty tomb on the third day. They saw him in resurrected glory. They saw him lovingly restore Peter.

So impressed by the love of God in Christ was John, that John would later write, "We know what real love is because Jesus gave up his life for us" (1 John 3:16 NLT). And he'd write, "God showed how much he loved us by sending his one and only Son into the world so that we might have eternal life through him. This is real love—not that we loved God, but that he loved us and sent his Son as a sacrifice to take away our sins" (1 John 4:9-10 NLT).

Likewise, *the church is the congregation that confronts the tension by being compelled by Christ's love.* We assert that God demonstrated "his own love for us in this: While we were still sinners, Christ died for us" (Romans 5:8). We can assert that no one has loved us like he has. No one has cared for us the way that he has. No one has taken the steps for us that he has. Nobody but Jesus took our sins, bore our sorrows, carried our griefs, faced the wrath that should have come to us, died our death, and faced our hell. Nobody but Jesus saw us at our worst and still loved us with his best and gave himself for us. We know nothing shall separate us from his love.

Who shall separate us from the love of Christ? Shall trouble or hardship or persecution or famine or nakedness or danger or sword? . . . No, in all these things we are more than conquerors through him who loved us. For I am convinced that neither death nor life, neither angels nor demons, neither the present nor the future, nor any powers, neither height nor depth, nor anything else in all creation, will be able to separate us from the love of God that is in Christ Jesus our Lord. (Romans 8:35-39)

I'm compelled by the height of his love, by the depth of his love, by the width of his love, by the strength of his love, by the flexibility of his love, by the specificity of his love. Therefore, I'll face the tension, because I have an experience with him. I'm compelled by his love. Like the song says, "Jesus loves me, this I know, for the Bible tells me so. Little ones to him belong, they are weak but he is strong. Yes, Jesus loves me."

12

HOW GOD'S PEOPLE PRAY

Then they called them in again and commanded them not to speak or teach at all in the name of Jesus. But Peter and John replied, "Which is right in God's eyes: to listen to you, or to him? You be the judges! As for us, we cannot help speaking about what we have seen and heard."

After further threats they let them go. They could not decide how to punish them, because all the people were praising God for what had happened. For the man who was miraculously healed was over forty years old.

On their release, Peter and John went back to their own people and reported all that the chief priests and the elders had said to them. When they heard this, they raised their voices together in prayer to God. "Sovereign Lord," they said, "you made the heavens and the earth and the sea, and everything in them. You spoke by the Holy Spirit through the mouth of your servant, our father David:

"'Why do the nations rage
    and the peoples plot in vain?

The kings of the earth rise up
    and the rulers band together
against the Lord
    and against his anointed one.'

"Indeed Herod and Pontius Pilate met together with the
Gentiles and the people of Israel in this city to conspire
against your holy servant Jesus, whom you anointed.
They did what your power and will had decided
beforehand should happen. Now, Lord, consider their
threats and enable your servants to speak your word
with great boldness. Stretch out your hand to heal and
perform signs and wonders through the name of your
holy servant Jesus."

After they prayed, the place where they were meeting
was shaken. And they were all filled with the Holy Spirit
and spoke the word of God boldly. (Acts 4:18-31)

Standing before the Sanhedrin Council and being le-
gally commanded to no longer speak or teach in Jesus'
name, Peter and John respond to the tension created by
their commitment to Jesus by asserting the integrity of
their experience with Jesus. They can't help but speak
what they've seen with their own eyes and have heard
with their own ears. From this, we learned that the church
lives within and confronts the tension created by its
commitment to Christ by asserting the integrity of

its experience with Christ and by being compelled by Christ's love.

Having issued their command and having received Peter and John's reply, the Sanhedrin let them go. Peter and John immediately return to the gathering of the saints and share their report. Upon hearing the report from Peter and John, which included the threats, they all begin to pray. Prayer was their automatic response. They put the matter into the hands of God.

The church is the fellowship that confronts threatening circumstances knowing the terrain of its struggle. The people understood that this was a spiritual struggle and they must confront it on the level of the spirit. Therefore, praying to God was their first response rather than their last resort. They did not seek to confront the Sanhedrin. They moved to consult God. They did so out of a particular understanding.

UNDERSTANDING THE GOD WE PRAY TO

The church prays out of an understanding of who God is. In Hebrews 11:6, we are told, "And without faith it is impossible to please God, because anyone who comes to him must believe that he exists and that he rewards those who earnestly seek him." Before there can be prayer, there must be a knowledge of God that produces a belief in God. We must know that God is and who God is. The two are not the same. I can know *that* someone is and still not know *who* that person is. Just knowing that someone is without knowing who the someone is, is not enough to create a relationship of belief and trust. It is in knowing *who* the person is that I can begin to know what is possible with them.

The church begins its prayer from the standpoint of to whom they are speaking. Listen to the words: "Sovereign Lord, . . . you made the heavens and the earth and the sea, and everything in them" (Acts 4:24). They aren't talking to just anybody. They are talking to the Sovereign Lord, the one who is in control. He's the one on the throne. He rules and super rules. He is the one to whom the nations are a drop in the bucket. He is the Sovereign Lord, the I Am that I Am. He is the Creator of the heavens and the earth, the sea and everything in them. He is the one who from nothing and no place spoke everything and every place into existence. He is the reason why whatever exists, has existed, and continues to exist. Light pierces the darkness because of him. Dry land appears from the midst of the waters because of him. Mountains stand forth being girded with power because of him. Birds assault the blue ether because of him. Fish navigate the oceans because of him. Constellations of stars illumine the canopy of the night because of him.

They pray to God because they know who he is. He is God and God all by himself. The earth is his, the fullness thereof, the world and they that dwell therein.

Having been threatened by creatures, they don't go to another creature; they go to the Creator. The creature is not greater than the Creator. The Creator holds the life of the creature in his hands. As the Creator, he can handle the Sanhedrin. Their times are in his hands.

The church prays out of a knowledge of who God is. When we know who God is, prayer comes easily. When we know that God is sovereign, prayer comes easily. When we know that God is Lord, prayer comes easily. When we know that God is the Creator of all, the sustainer of all, and master of all, prayer comes easily. We say to ourselves, "I refuse to believe that my struggles and my troubles are bigger, greater, stronger than my God."

PRAYING OUT OF WHAT GOD HAS SAID

The church also prays out of an understanding of what God has said. Verse 24 portrays their praying out of knowing who God is, but verse 25 reveals them addressing what God said. They continue praying,

> You spoke by the Holy Spirit through the mouth of your servant, our father David:
>
> > "'Why do the nations rage
> >   and the peoples plot in vain?
> > The kings of the earth rise up
> >   and the rulers band together
> > against the Lord
> >   and against his anointed one.'
>
> "Indeed Herod and Pontius Pilate met together with the Gentiles and the people of Israel in this city to

conspire against your holy servant Jesus, whom you anointed. They did what your power and will had decided beforehand should happen." (Acts 4:25-28)

They bring up what God said and the fact that God fulfilled his word. They make their current request to God based upon God having given a word and having fulfilled a word. They trusted that God will never turn from his word.

The church prays out of an understanding of the word of God. It puts God's word in front of God, not because God forgets what God says. It puts God's word before God as a display of taking God's word seriously. When we pray according to the word of God, we let God know that we take God's word seriously.

I've discovered that God gets excited when we take his word seriously. I believe that there are moments when God waits on us to take his word as seriously as he takes his word. I believe that God's ears are piqued just waiting for somebody to come to him with a belief in his word and to declare: *You said,* "Ask and it will be given to you; seek and you will find; knock and the door will be opened to you" (Matthew 7:7); "If you remain in me and my words remain in you, ask whatever you wish, and it will be done for you" (John 15:7). *You said,* "If my people, who are called by my name, will humble themselves and pray and seek my face and turn from their wicked ways, then I will hear from heaven, and I will forgive their sin and will heal their land" (2 Chronicles 7:14). *You said,* "I will rescue those who love me. I will protect those who trust in my name. When they call on me, I will answer; I will be with them in trouble. I will rescue them and honor them. I will reward them with a long life and show them my salvation" (Psalm 91:14-16 NLT). *God, you said I could call you when I need you. You said you would answer when I call you. You said you would supply all my needs according to your riches in glory.*

The church prays out of a knowledge of what God has said. I have no other reason to ask God to be with me, other than the fact that God said in his Word, "I am with you always, to the very end of the age" (Matthew 28:20); and

> Do not fear, for I have redeemed you; I have summoned you by name; you are mine. When you pass through the waters, I will be with you; and when you pass through the rivers, they will not sweep over you. When you walk through the fire, you will not be burned; the flames will not set you ablaze. (Isaiah 43:1-2)

Therefore, it doesn't matter what threats the Sanhedrin made, the church went to God based upon what God said. As the Sovereign Lord, God could use their threats and action to accomplish what God said. Joseph could testify:

> God said that I'd surpass my brothers and that they'd bow to me. That's what God said. My brothers sold me into Ishmaelite slavery. They lied and told my father that I was dead. But God took what they did and accomplished what God said. The Ishmaelites took me

into Egypt where I met Potiphar. Potiphar's wife lied on me. Potiphar put me in Pharaoh's prison. It was there that God developed my administrative and interpretive skills. It was there that I met Pharaoh's cupbearer who would connect me to Pharaoh. It was through that connection that God would put me where he put me to be able to save many who were alive. (Genesis 37, 39–41, author's paraphrase)

The church acknowledges it in their prayer. The heathens raged. Herod Antipas, Pontius Pilate, the Gentiles, and the people of Israel were all united against Jesus whom God anointed. But God used all that they did against Jesus to do what God said that he'd do with Jesus and for Jesus. God said that he'd put enmity between the seed of the woman and the seed of the serpent. God said that he'd send a redeemer who'd be wounded for our transgressions, bruised for our iniquities, chastened for our peace, and have stripes for our healing. God used what they did against Jesus to accomplish what God said that he'd do with Jesus.

That's good news. God is the God who can use what people do against us to accomplish what he said that he'd do for us and with us. Knowing that, the church prayed and declared that they would stand on the Word. Regardless of the threats, we're standing on the Word. Regardless of the predictions, we're standing on the Word. Regardless of the forecasts, we're standing on the Word.

ASKING FOR BOLDNESS

The church affirms who God is. God is the God who does just what he says. They don't ask God to lessen the threats; they ask God to increase their boldness. *The church is the body of people who respond to the tension created by their commitment to Jesus by seeking increased boldness.* Facing the boldness of the Sanhedrin, they seek the boldness of God. They seek the courage of God. Their failure would not be a failure of knowledge. It would be a failure of courage. They needed the boldness of God to overcome their fear.

The church is the body that must forever be found seeking God for boldness. The times in which we live are times that test the courage that we have. The world is bold in its assertions. Extremists of every kind are bold in their assertions. The church of the Lord Jesus Christ must be bold in its declaration. To those who boldly want to minimize, marginalize, and make peripheral the proclamation of the gospel of Jesus Christ, believers must be heard boldly declaring the centrality, the uniqueness, the singularity of Jesus Christ. To those who boldly assert that ethnic and racial minorities don't belong in the United States, who boldly propagate a philosophy of hate, the church must be heard boldly, uniformly, and unequivocally declaring such positions to be ungodly, sinful, and having no place within either the fabric of American society or fabric of Christian faith. We need a boldness that defies political calculation and public opinion.

They prayed for boldness in their preaching and for healing power, miraculous signs, and wonders done through the name of Jesus Christ. Now, lest we rush too quickly, we'll miss where the emphasis is. Most would put the emphasis on the matter of boldness, miracles, and healing. That's not where the emphasis is. The emphasis is on the words *through the name of Jesus*. They were threatened, even ordered, against speaking or teaching in the name of Jesus. This was done to negate Jesus. It was done to stifle the Jesus movement, to nip the Jesus message in the bud.

The church prays that God give it boldness and send healing power, miraculous signs, and wonders through the name of Jesus.

PRAYING TO EXALT JESUS' NAME

The main concern of their prayer was the name of Jesus. They want the name of Jesus to be exalted and glorified. Against the desire to lessen, to lower, to diminish, to disparage the name of Jesus, they pray for God to expand the name, highlight the name, honor the name, legitimate the name of Jesus.

The church seeks God's answer to prayer as a means of advancing the name of Jesus. For these early believers, the particulars of their prayer had one aim; the advancement of the name of Jesus. This was a Jesus thing. Whenever God sees a concern for the advancement of the kingdom, when God hears a concern for his name, God gets excited. Luke records that as they were praying, the building began to shake

(Acts 4:31). God began to shake some things up; he demonstrated that the earth belonged to him in a tangible way. They were all filled afresh with the Holy Spirit and preached the word of God with boldness. Great witness was given concerning the resurrection of Jesus. When there is a concern for the claim and fame of God, God gets excited. In John 12 when Jesus prays, "Now my soul is troubled, and what shall I say? 'Father save me from this hour'? No, it was for this very reason I came to this hour. Father, glorify your name!" (v. 27-28), God responds with an audible voice from heaven saying, " I have glorified it, and will glorify it again" (v. 28).

God responded with Jesus at Calvary. He responded with Jesus in resurrection.

With great boldness, the church preached the word of God. They advanced the name of Jesus. Against the threats of the Sanhedrin, they advanced the name of Jesus. Against the opposition of Rome, they advanced the name of Jesus. Throughout the ages, the name of Jesus has been advanced. And here we are, still advancing the name of Jesus. It still is the only name given whereby we must be saved. It still is the saving and redeeming name. It still is the delivering name. It still is the healing name. It still is the providing name. When we speak his name, something happens. When we call his name, he will come to us. Demons tremble. Sickness flees. Heaven responds.

13

TOGETHER IN EVERYTHING

> After they prayed, the place where they were meeting was shaken. And they were all filled with the Holy Spirit and spoke the word of God boldly.
>
> All the believers were one in heart and mind. No one claimed that any of their possessions was their own, but they shared everything they had. With great power the apostles continued to testify to the resurrection of the Lord Jesus. And God's grace was so powerfully at work in them all that there were no needy persons among them. For from time to time those who owned land or houses sold them, brought the money from the sales and put it at the apostles' feet, and it was distributed to anyone who had need.
>
> Joseph, a Levite from Cyprus, whom the apostles called Barnabas (which means "son of encouragement"), sold a field he owned and brought the money and put it at the apostles' feet. (Acts 4:31-37)

Having been threatened against speaking or teaching in the name of Jesus, the church prays for boldness in proclamation and God's powerful works of demonstration through the name of Jesus. God responded with a move that shook the building, filled them afresh with the Holy Spirit, and emboldened them to preach the word of God, that bore witness to the resurrection of Jesus.

While under threat, the church was at its best. They were united in heart and in mind. They shared everything that they had. The apostles testified to the resurrection. God's blessing was on them all.

THE CHURCH AT ITS BEST

The pressure that was designed to limit, curb, stifle, and still them and their work only served to draw them closer to God who empowered them to be at their best.

The church is the body of believers whose relationship with God empowers them to face the worst and show the best. Peter and John faced the same group that engineered the mistrial and crucifixion of Jesus. Then they were temporarily jailed and later placed under religious legal injunction against speaking or teaching in the name of Jesus. They report both experiences to the members of the fellowship. This is the worst that they had experienced since Jesus' ascension.

However, it doesn't result in their toning down or closing shop. It doesn't lead to mass departures from the fold. Instead, it results in united prayer, communal empowerment, increased proclamation of and witness to the resurrection of Jesus, and cooperative economic activity. While facing the worst, the church was at its best.

The power of a relationship with God is often demonstrated when things are at their worst. When life is good and things are easy, not much is required of you. It doesn't take much to smile, to be nice, to stick, to stay. It's when things shift, when life goes left, when pressure comes, when threats arise, when diagnoses are given—that's when the challenge comes. Who are we and how are we then? How together are we? How bold are we? How committed are we? How loving are we? How consistent are we? How cooperative are we? How supportive are we? How generous are we then?

Threatened with the worst, their relationship with Christ empowers them to display their best. A relationship with Christ empowers us to face the worst and display the best. We can get the worst news like Job and still worship God, declaring, "The LORD gave and the LORD has taken away; may the name of the LORD be praised" (Job 1:21). With the threat of no figs on the vine, the olive trees failing, and no herds in the stall, a relationship with God moves us to declare, "Yet will I rejoice . . . in the God of my salvation" (Habakkuk 3:18 NKJV).

There is something about knowing God that makes possible the displaying of the best of us in the worst of times. It's the capacity for the best of us to be seen in the worst of situations. There is a luminescence in God that can only be seen when things get dark.

For years, our family has visited Epcot at Disney to ride the rides. We usually have gone during the day. We would ride the rides, eat lunch, and go home. Recently, we went in the evening. We went to the same rides, ate dinner and walked the same paths—but one thing was different for me. As we were walking and I looked down, there were these intricately drawn illuminated patterns in the sidewalk; they were drawn into the sidewalk. They were there during the day, but I didn't see them because they only light up at night. The pattern is there during the day, but the power shines at night. There is a luminescence in God that can be seen best when things are at their worst.

RESPONSIBILITY FOR EACH OTHER

The church is at its best when its relational connectedness leads to members assuming responsibility for each other. Core to the formation and functioning of the church was relational connectedness. They were called to be the body together. They were developed and sent out for field education in fellowship (Mark 6:7); they received the revelation of the resurrection in fellowship (Mark 16:9-14); they were commissioned in fellowship (Matthew 28:16-20); they witnessed the ascension in fellowship (Luke 24:50-53); they were filled by the Spirit in fellowship (Acts 2:1-4); and they bore witness to the truth of the Gospel in fellowship (Acts 2:14-16, 37).

In the midst of the threats of the Sanhedrin, they maintained their relational connectedness. All of them were united in heart and mind. They did not splinter or disintegrate. They held fast and stood fast. They drew close and stayed close. They continued meeting together and breaking bread from house to house. Their fellowship, their relational connectedness was an identifying characteristic. They were known for their fellowship.

The church is at its best when its relational connectedness is evident. Its life together empowers it to be at its best. The day and age in which we live desperately calls for a renewed understanding and appreciation for the relational connectedness of the church. We must reaffirm the truth of what authentic Christian community is. In his book *Life Together*, Dietrich Bonhoeffer asserts that, "Christian community means community through Jesus Christ and in Jesus Christ." Flowing from this is the realization that "a Christian needs others for the sake of Jesus Christ. It means, second, that a Christian comes to others only through Jesus Christ. It means, third, that from eternity we have been chosen in Jesus Christ, accepted in time, and united for eternity."[1] Our growth and maturity in Christ is tied to our personal involvement and investment in the community of believers. It is in the context of Christian community and fellowship that believers are called out of a selfishness and called into a selflessness for others.

The church is at its best when its relational connectedness leads to its members assuming responsibility for each other. A reading of the text reveals that those who gathered were responsible to and for each other. Beginning in Acts 2, Luke tells us,

> And all the believers met together in one place and shared everything they had. They sold their property and possessions and shared the money with those in need. They worshiped together at the Temple each day, met in homes for the Lord's Supper, and shared their meals with great joy and generosity. (vv. 44-46 NLT)

The threats of the Sanhedrin didn't deter their practice.

> All the believers were united in heart and mind. And they felt that what they owned was not their own, so they shared everything they had. . . . There were no needy people among them, because those who owned land or houses would sell them and bring the money to the apostles to give to those in need. (Acts 4:32, 34-35 NLT)

Their connectedness tied them together in such a way that each person felt responsible to and for everyone else.

There was a day and age when this was so. Back when access to other things and places was denied to us—when the church was all that we had—being responsible to and for each other was easy because it was necessary. With the perceived opening of access to other opportunities, the necessity of communal responsibility to and for each other diminished. Another factor in the diminishing of communal responsibility is the advent of the church being seen more as a religious programming center, similar to a retail shopping center where people look for their grocery lists of spiritual needs to be met without having to invest any of themselves into the life and livelihood of the church. Where and when the church simply becomes the context for me to get my word for the week, I will not place myself in a position to be responsible to or for anyone.

Such a posture runs counter to biblical expectation and practice of the church. It is important to note that Paul wrote to communities of faith who were facing challenges to their relational connectedness. He wrote:

Don't just pretend to love others. Really love them. Hate what is wrong. Hold tightly to what is good. Love each other with genuine affection, and take delight in honoring each other. (Romans 12:9-10 NLT)

Get rid of all bitterness, rage, anger, harsh words, and slander, as well as all types of evil behavior. Instead, be kind to each other, tenderhearted, forgiving one another, just as God through Christ has forgiven you. (Ephesians 4:31-32 NLT)

Is there any encouragement from belonging to Christ? Any comfort from his love? Any fellowship together in the Spirit? Are your hearts tender and compassionate? Then make me truly happy by agreeing wholeheartedly with each other, loving one another,

and working together with one mind and purpose.
Don't be selfish; don't try to impress others. Be
humble, thinking of others as better than yourselves.
. . . but take an interest in others, too. (Philippians 2:1-4 NLT)

Each were being encouraged to do their part in the maintenance and strengthening of those ties.

As each letter was read within the worship settings, the
members were being challenged to rise up to their individual responsibility to and for each other. It was not about
what they expected to be done for them. It was what they
were expected to do for each other.

SHARING EVERYTHING

The church is at its best when members see what they possess
as something to pass through them rather than being held by
them. In both Acts 2:44 and Acts 4:32, a note is mentioned about their stewardship. Before the threats of the
Sanhedrin, Luke notes that they shared everything that
they had, and after the threats of the Sanhedrin, he notes
that they shared everything that they had. The changing
of the climate did not change their stewardship orien-
tation. Facing less pressure or more pressure did not
change how they viewed their relationship with their possessions. The picture is one where no one exhibited selfishness or possessiveness. They shared without the
thought of reciprocity. They did not view the use of their

money being simply for themselves. They saw it also for the blessing of others.

The church is at its best when members see what they possess as something to pass through them rather than to be hoarded by them. It is an approach to material possessions as a trust from God to be used for his purposes, which includes the blessing of others. It is the loose holding of things such that we can let them go whenever letting go is needed. The knowledge of needs is always a time for loose holding so that we can let it go for the benefit of others.

Such was the case for the church at Philippi and Macedonia. Paul speaks of them in 2 Corinthians 8. He writes,

> Now I want you to know, dear brothers and sisters, what God in his kindness has done through the churches in Macedonia. They are being tested by many troubles, and they are very poor. But they are also filled with abundant joy, which has overflowed in rich generosity.
>
> For I can testify that they gave not only what they could afford, but far more. And they did it of their own free will. They begged us again and again for the privilege of sharing in the gift for the believers in Jerusalem. (2 Corinthians 8:1-4 NLT)

The church is at its best when its members take responsibility for responding to recognized needs. There were those who owned land or houses. Whenever a need was lifted, these individuals would sell some of their holdings in order to meet the particular need.

WORKING TOGETHER

The church is at its best when members realize that the collective body can only accomplish what the individual members participate in making happen. The body only functions by the proper functioning and participation of the members. The body walks only by the brain sending the signal, the central nervous system carrying the signal, the muscles, tendons, sinews, joints, ligaments, and bones all properly functioning. If one of them does not function, walking does not happen. Movement does not take place. The body is at its best when each member of the body does its own special work.

Luke highlights the actions of one of those members. He is a Levite named Joseph, who was nicknamed Barnabas— we'll look more closely at his story in chapter fourteen. On one occasion, he sold a field that he owned and brought the money to the apostles (Acts 4:36-37). His being in relational connection informed him of a need within the body. His relational connection impressed on him the individual responsibility that he had; something must come from him. He couldn't sit this one out. He couldn't wait for someone else to respond. He must step up to the plate. He must get into the game. The need would be met by him. The challenge to him was to make who he was and what he possessed available. The response of the body depended upon him making who he was and what he possessed available. The strength of the body's response was dependent upon the strength of his response. The immediacy of the body's response was contingent upon the immediacy of his response.

The church is at its best when the members operate out of the realization that the church can only do what the members bring themselves to do. The church can only respond as swiftly and as strongly as the members' participation empowers it to respond. The missional and programmatic thrust will only be as impactful as the members bring themselves to have meaningful impact.

Barnabas responded by bringing who he was and what he possessed and laid it at the apostles' feet. Barnabas placed who he was and what he possessed at the Lord's disposal looking for nothing in return, because he had already received everything from the Lord. He brought his best to the Lord who already had given him his best.

If we want to see the church at its best, those who make up the church must be willing to put who they are and what they possess at the Lord's disposal. There must be a placing of time at the Lord's disposal, talent at the Lord's disposal, treasure at the Lord's disposal, skills at the Lord's disposal, resources at the Lord's disposal, contacts at the Lord's disposal, connections at the Lord's disposal, experiences at the Lord's disposal, exposure at the Lord's disposal.

When we do so, we meet God and Jesus at their best. Whatever we are and whatever we possess, it's because God placed it at our disposal. The breath that we take, the health that we have, the strength that we have, the minds that we have, the intelligence that we have, the charisma that we have, the ability that we have, the opportunities that we have, the reach that we have, the influence that we have, all come from him. More important than any and all of these things is the salvation that we have. It came from God who did not hold anything back. For God so loved the world that he gave his only begotten Son. He freely gave his only Son. Jesus freely gave his life; no one took his life. He had power to lay it down and power to raise it up again. He freely gave his body to be broken. He freely gave his blood to be shed. He freely sacrificed himself on our behalf. At Calvary, we see him at his best. Against the ugliness of Calvary, we see the beauty of God at its best. Against hatred of Calvary, we see the love of God at its best. Against the darkness of Calvary, we see the light of God at its best. In fact it is at the cross where we first see the light. Against the death at Calvary, we see the life of God at its best on the third day morning when God raises Jesus from the dead.

I saw him at his best. I came to him at my worst, but I found him at his best. Now, I'm determined to meet his best with my best. I challenge us to meet the Lord's best with our best. Let's all together meet him with our best. I challenge us to bring who we are and what we possess to him, to place who we are and what we have at his disposal.

14

THE CHURCH AT ITS WORST

All the believers were united in heart and mind. And they felt that what they owned was not their own, so they shared everything they had. The apostles testified powerfully to the resurrection of the Lord Jesus, and God's great blessing was upon them all. There were no needy people among them, because those who owned land or houses would sell them and bring the money to the apostles to give to those in need.

For instance, there was Joseph, the one the apostles nicknamed Barnabas (which means "Son of Encouragement"). He was from the tribe of Levi and came from the island of Cyprus. He sold a field he owned and brought the money to the apostles.

But there was a certain man named Ananias who, with his wife, Sapphira, sold some property. He brought part of the money to the apostles, claiming it was the full amount. With his wife's consent, he kept the rest.

Then Peter said, "Ananias, why have you let Satan fill your heart? You lied to the Holy Spirit, and you kept some of the money for yourself. The property was yours to sell or not sell, as you wished. And after selling it, the money was also yours to give away. How could you do a thing like this? You weren't lying to us but to God!"

As soon as Ananias heard these words, he fell to the floor and died. Everyone who heard about it was terrified. Then some young men got up, wrapped him in a sheet, and took him out and buried him.

About three hours later his wife came in, not knowing what had happened. Peter asked her, "Was this the price you and your husband received for your land?"

"Yes," she replied, "that was the price."

And Peter said, "How could the two of you even think of conspiring to test the Spirit of the Lord like this? The young men who buried your husband are just outside the door, and they will carry you out, too."

Instantly, she fell to the floor and died. When the young men came in and saw that she was dead, they carried her out and buried her beside her husband. Great fear gripped the entire church and everyone else who heard what had happened.

The apostles were performing many miraculous signs and wonders among the people. And all the believers were meeting regularly at the Temple in the area known as Solomon's Colonnade. But no one else dared to join them, even though all the people had high regard for them. Yet more and more people believed and were brought to the Lord—crowds of both men and women. (Acts 4:32–5:14 NLT)

With our last chapter, we were able to see the church facing the worst and showing the best. Under legal injunction against speaking or teaching the name and person of Jesus, the church was united in heart and mind. They shared everything that they had. The apostles testified to the resurrection. God's blessing was upon them all. We discovered that the church is at its best when its relational connectedness leads to members assuming responsibility for each other; when members see what they possess as something to pass through them rather than being held by them; and when members realize that the collective body can only accomplish what the individual members participate in making happen.

Luke provided a specific example of one of the members of the church making things happen. His name is Joseph, a Levite from the town of Cyprus. Upon hearing of the need within the church, he sells a piece of property and brings the full proceeds to the apostles for the meeting of the need. He brings who he is and what he has and places it at the Lord's disposal. We concluded with the realization that the church will only be at its best when those who make up the church are willing to put who they are and what they possess at the Lord's disposal.

In response to Joseph's actions, the apostles nickname him Barnabas, "Son of Encouragement." His parents gave him the name Joseph. His lifestyle earned him the name Barnabas. From our engagement and involvement within the gathered body of the church, what name have we earned? If we were to die, what has our engagement and involvement given someone to say about us? What adjective or descriptive could be used to honestly nickname us?

For his service, for his sacrifice, Joseph the Levite from Cyprus is nicknamed Barnabas, "Son of Encouragement." With that, the chapter closes, to be followed by another chapter in the church's story. There are many ways that the next chapter could begin. It could begin with words like *and*, *also*, *in addition to*, *therefore*, or *as a result of*. Instead, the continuation of the story begins with the word *but*. This word is a contrastive and super-ordinating conjunction. Simply put, it is a word that suggests an oppositional thought or relationship to what was previously stated that is more significant than what was previously stated. This word suggests that as powerful as the previous statement was, pay attention to what follows because its power is greater, and its weight is heavier.

There are occasions when this is a good thing. Occasions like "Weeping may endure for a night, but joy comes in the morning" (Psalm 30:5 NKJV) and "We are . . . perplexed, but not in despair; persecuted, but not abandoned; struck down, but not destroyed" (2 Corinthians 4:8-10). In the case of this text, the word *but* does not carry a very hopeful or positive meaning. Its presence in this instance suggests an experience that is quite different from that of Barnabas.

It begins with the words, "But there was a certain man named Ananias who, with his wife, Sapphira . . ." (Acts 5:1 NLT). With chapter four ending with the powerfully positive example of Barnabas, chapter five begins with the word *but* followed by the names of two other members of the church, suggesting an opposite and more weighty story.

THE OTHER SIDE OF THE COIN

Just as the church is seen at its best through its members so also is the church seen at its worst through its members. The story could have continued with the word *and*. Instead, it reads *but* due to the choice and action of Ananias and Sapphira. From this, we come to realize that each member is responsible for how the story of the church reads. Each member's actions or lack thereof adds either an *and* or a *but*. When one member shows hospitality to guests, every other member's actions add either an *and* or a *but* to the experience. When one member brings the tithe and sacrificial offering, every other member's actions add either an *and* or a *but* to the giving story. When a group of people gives themselves to the study life of the church, every other member's actions add either an *and* or a *but* to the discipling story of the church. When some people invite people to church and share their faith, every other member's actions add either an *and* or a *but* to the church's evangelistic story. If Luke were writing about us in the story of the church, would he use the word *and* or *but* in describing us in the study life, serving life, sharing life, and sacrificing life of the church?

Chapter five starts: "But there was a certain man named Ananias who, with his wife, Sapphira, sold some property. He brought part of the money to the apostles, claiming it was the full amount. With his wife's consent, he kept the rest" (vv. 1-2 NLT). As Joseph the Levite is being heralded as Barnabas the son of encouragement by the apostles, two members of the church are there. They are a husband and wife team. Like Barnabas, they sell a piece of property that they own. Ananias brings part of the money to the apostles, claiming that what he brings is the full amount of the sale. Luke alerts us that he keeps the rest and that he does this with the consent of his wife.

As Ananias presents it to the apostles, Peter confronts him saying, "Why have you let Satan fill your heart? You lied to the Holy Spirit , and you kept some of the money for yourself. The property was yours to sell or not sell, as you wished. And after selling it, the money was also yours to give away. How could you do a thing like this? You weren't lying to us but to God!" (vv. 3-4 NLT). As soon as those words are spoken and heard, Ananias falls dead to the ground. Fear strikes the crowd that witnesses it. Some people wrap Ananias's body and bury him in a nearby field.

About three hours later, Sapphira comes to the worship gathering. Unaware of what has happened, she's operating under what she and Ananias had agreed to. Peter questions her about the price that they received for the land being the amount that they had given. She answers that it was. To which Peter says, "How could the two of you even think of conspiring to test the Spirit of the Lord like this? The young men who buried your husband are just outside the door, and they will carry you out, too" (v. 9 NLT). Like Ananias, she falls dead to the ground, whereupon she is carried and buried beside her husband.

Right after seeing the church at its best through the actions of a member, we see the church at its worst through the actions of two members. Just as the church is seen at its best through its members, so also is the church seen at its worst through its members. This is an important truth: The completion and perfection of the church is ultimately found and guaranteed by one person and one person alone—Jesus. The current imperfection and inconsistency experienced in every church is guaranteed by its members. Whether it is a church of ten or ten thousand, we will find imperfection and inconsistency in every church. The reason why is that every person who is a member of any church is imperfect and inconsistent. Just look at the initial twelve who were put together after a night of prayer. Every one of them imperfect and inconsistent. There is no place that we can go where there will not be imperfection and inconsistency. If by some miracle there was a perfect church, the moment that we joined would make it imperfect and inconsistent because we are imperfect and inconsistent. Our perfection and completion are in Christ. God has established the church, the gathered fellowship of believers, to be the context where we are developed, where we are grown, where we become more complete through what we each provide to the other.

With Ananias and Sapphira, we see the church at its worst. It is such an alarming sight that they both are struck dead and buried. This is the first double funeral of the church. There are sobering warnings that God issues to the church in this episode.

SELFISH CONCERN

The church is at its worst when its members' selfish concerns make them vulnerable to satanic influence. When the church faced the external attack of persecution, Barnabas showed its best; but Satan attacks the church from within by Ananias and Sapphira showing its worst. Peter quickly identifies Satan's presence in the midst. He asks Ananias, "Why have you let Satan fill your heart?" Peter identifies Ananias as operating with a heart full of the devil. Though Ananias is not ranting, raging, foaming at the mouth, head spinning around, or talking in a scary voice, Peter identifies his heart being under Satan's influence. He's in church, giving money, yet full of the devil. Externally,

Ananias and Sapphira appear to be operating under the holiest of motives, but internally, they are operating under the influence of Satan himself.

Peter recognizes it and calls it out because he's experienced being called out himself. In Matthew 16, right after Peter confesses Jesus to be the Christ, the Son of the Living God, Jesus rebukes Peter for operating under satanic influence. When Jesus began to share that he would suffer and be crucified, Peter sought to deny what Jesus was saying. In Matthew 16:23-24, Jesus responded saying, "Get behind me, Satan! You are a stumbling block to me; you do not have in mind the concerns of God, but merely human concerns." Then Jesus said to the disciples, "Whoever wants to be my disciple must deny themselves and take up their cross and follow me." Peter recognized that the selfish ambition of Ananias and Sapphira had opened them up to be influenced by the devil himself. He calls it out.

The only way that Satan can attack the church from within is if someone from within gives him a ride. The way in which Satan is given a ride within the church is through the self-centered concerns and ambitions of members. Satan's subtlety is his manipulating something that concerns the self. He inflames a thought, a feeling, a desire, an aim, a fear that resides within the heart. With seemingly the smallest and most innocent of openings, he enters with the intent to kill, steal, and destroy. His genius is that he doesn't manufacture anything new. He just uses what is alive within us. That is why you can be full of him and not know it because he hopped a ride on what you're full of. Look at him manipulate the desire of Eve for interaction, for knowledge, for equal status with God. Look at him manipulate Adam's desire for Eve. Look at him manipulate James and John's desire for position to stir up division in the camp. Look at him inflame Judas's disappointment in Jesus to move Judas to betray Jesus.

For Ananias and Sapphira, it was a combination of envy and pride. As they saw Joseph the Levite being lauded for his generosity, they desired it for themselves. Like Joseph, they were property owners of some means. Whatever attention that they saw him get, whatever reputation that they saw him establish, they wanted also. Satan begins to water that seed and manipulate their thoughts and feelings. Can you hear the internal conversation? Don't the apostles know who they are, what they have to offer? Barnabas isn't the only one who can write a check. We can write a check too. Somebody better recognize.

The church is at its worst when its members' selfish concerns make them vulnerable to satanic influence.

Satan inflames Ananias and Sapphira's self-concern into a plot for self-promotion. The church is at its worst when its members are more concerned about the promotion of self than the glory of God. While Barnabas's actions came out of a concern for the meeting of the need and the fulfilling of the ministry vision, Ananias and Sapphira would act for the promotion of themselves. This would be for them and about them.

It is an unfortunate thing that, for many, engagement and involvement in the church is reduced to it being for them and about them. While what they do is in a religious setting, what they do has more to do with them than with God. It is more about the promotion of them, the fulfillment of them, the furtherance of them than it is anything else. If they are not getting what they perceive that they deserve from it or through it, they have no use or time for it.

With a desire to promote themselves, these two hatch the scheme of selling a piece of property and giving part of the proceeds under the guise of it being the full amount of the sale. Here we see the character of Satan in what they do; Satan is the great deceiver. Ananias and Sapphira employ deception to appear to be more than who they are and to do more than what they did. They want to appear to be like Barnabas and to be doing what Barnabas did without actually doing what he did. They want the reputation and commendation for being sacrificial without the actual sacrifice.

Peter speaks to this. Again, listen to him, "Ananias, why have you let Satan fill your heart? You lied to the Holy Spirit, and you kept some of the money for yourself. The property was yours to sell or not sell. . . . And after selling it, the money was also yours to give away. How could you do a thing like this? You weren't lying to us but to God!" (Acts 5:3-4 NLT). Peter does not confront Ananias about keeping some of the money for himself, he confronts him about claiming that what he gave was the whole of what he received. It was his claiming to be who he wasn't and to have done what he didn't do.

STATUS AND APPEARANCE

Ananias claimed to be unselfishly devoted and completely sold out to God, when in reality, he was more concerned about his recognition and status.

The church is at its worst when its members are more concerned about appearance than actuality. Ananias and Sapphira's desire to appear to be more than they were was greater than their desire to become more than they were. Appearing to be and authentically being are two different things. For some, so much of life is lived by way of appearance and not reality. That presents a problem when it comes to a relationship with Christ. A relationship with Christ is not about his power to make you appear to be different, but to actually be different. Christ comes to us not to put some spiritual makeup on us in an attempt to beautify the old self. Christ comes into our lives to empower us to put off the old self and to take on a brand-new self that doesn't need makeup. Christ comes into our lives not for us to appear to be loving, but to actually be loving; not to appear to be generous, but to actually be generous;

not to appear to be kind, but to actually be kind. Crossing the gap between appearance and actuality will always require more of us and from us than we are comfortable giving up.

Ananias and Sapphira would have done better simply by honestly presenting what they gave as a part of what they received. Here was the lie of Satan; they needed to appear to be more in order to be accepted and valued. Under the influence of their envy and pride and inflamed by a lie of Satan, they did not understand that what they gave would have been appreciated if they had just been honest with what it was. Integrity is owning who you are and where you are. Integrity is not labeling something as a tithe when it isn't the tithe. If it's less than the tenth, integrity is labeling whatever it is as an offering or donation.

Perhaps the inner conflict with knowing what level they should be on prompted them to present themselves as being where they weren't. The problem is that presenting themselves as being where they weren't did not result in their being where they weren't.

Peter charges them with lying to the Holy Spirit. They were not acting in truth. The identity of the one to whom they lied was not Peter or the church. They were lying to God and the Holy Spirit. Therefore, the only people that they were fooling were themselves.

All eyes are on Ananias as he presents his offering to Peter. People are ready to celebrate Ananias for his generosity and sacrifice. Then Peter calls him out as one whose heart Satan had filled. Had Peter not said anything, no one would ever have thought of Ananias and Sapphira in those terms. But Peter does call them out on it.

WHOSE APPROVAL DO YOU WANT?

In calling them out on it, he confronts them with their concern about people. *The church is at its worst where the praise of men means more than the approval of God.* Ananias and Sapphira were so concerned about how people would look at them that they failed to consider how God would look at them. They failed to understand how God already saw them. They bought into the lie that they had to do something to appear to be more than who they were. They didn't realize that who they were in Christ did not require them to appear to be anything other than who they were. Their misplaced focus on people prompted them to take action that failed to properly focus on God. Peter gives them a chance to come clean and repent. They both continue perpetrating a fraud rather than coming clean. Had they just come clean, forgiveness could be found. Had they just come clean, another chance could be given.

The desire for appearance before people can leave us in a spot we never imagined. The fear and reverence for God must take priority over the concern for people. God strikes both of them dead. This is a radical step for God to take. One writer has suggested that God makes the point that

God does not cease to be holy simply because he is gracious and loving. Therefore, we are not to presume on the graciousness and love of God believing that there are no lines that he does not draw and no consequences that he does not enforce.

They are both struck dead. With that, Luke writes, "Great fear gripped the entire church" (Acts 5:11 NLT). The word for *fear* in this instance refers to the response that comes after encountering a force that is greater than we are. God's actions against Ananias and Sapphira result in the reestablishing of reverence for God. It put God back at the center. This is not about us, this is about him. This is about the acknowledgment of God that results in reverence and submission. It put the nature of their relationship back into focus. God is spirit and those who worship him must worship him in spirit and in truth. God rejects deceitful worship and vain worship.

God nips this in the bud at the beginning because he does not want people to be infected with the "disease of me." In his book titled *The Winner Within*, Pat Riley talks about the Los Angeles Lakers' 1980-81 season. Riley says, "Because of greed, pettiness, and resentment, we executed one of the fastest falls from grace in NBA history." It was the Disease of Me.[1]

God could not allow Ananias and Sapphira to spread the disease of me. With the church in its infancy, God doesn't want it shaped by a spirit of grasping, selfishness, envy, and deceit. He wants it to be shaped by the mind and spirit of his Son.

> Who, being in very nature God, did not consider equality with God something to be used to his own advantage; rather, he made himself nothing by taking the very nature of a servant, being made in human likeness. And being found in appearance as a man, he humbled himself by becoming obedient to death— even death on a cross!
>
> Therefore God exalted him to the highest place and gave him the name that is above every name, that at the name of Jesus every knee should bow, in heaven and on earth and under the earth, and every tongue acknowledge that Jesus Christ is Lord, to the glory of God the Father. (Philippians 2:6-11)

God wants a church infected by a love for him, a desire for him, a witness of him. Create a church at its best that wants God in actuality, that wants his character in actuality, that wants his will in actuality, that wants to serve him in actuality, that wants to please him in actuality.

15

GROWING INTO THE FUTURE

Now many signs and wonders were done among the people through the apostles. And they were all together in Solomon's Portico. None of the rest dared to join them, but the people held them in high esteem. Yet more than ever believers were added to the Lord, great numbers of both men and women, so that they even carried out the sick into the streets, and laid them on cots and mats, in order that Peter's shadow might fall on some of them as he came by. A great number of people would also gather from the towns around Jerusalem, bringing the sick and those tormented by unclean spirits, and they were all cured.

Then the high priest took action; he and all who were with him (that is, the sect of the Sadducees), being filled with jealousy, arrested the apostles and put them in the public prison. But during the night an angel of the Lord opened the prison doors, brought them out, and said, "Go, stand in the temple and tell the people the whole message about this life." When they heard this, they entered the temple at daybreak and went on with their teaching.

When the high priest and those with him arrived, they called together the council and the whole body of the elders of Israel, and sent to the prison to have them brought. But when the temple police went there, they did not find them in the prison; so they returned and reported, "We found the prison securely locked and the guards standing at the doors, but when we opened them, we found no one inside." Now when the captain of the temple and the chief priests heard these words, they were perplexed about them, wondering what might be going on. Then someone arrived and announced, "Look, the men whom you put in prison are standing in the temple and teaching the people!" Then the captain went with the temple police and brought them, but without violence, for they were afraid of being stoned by the people.

When they had brought them, they had them stand before the council. The high priest questioned them, saying, "We gave you strict orders not to teach in this name, yet here you have filled Jerusalem with your teaching and you are determined to bring this man's blood on us." But Peter and the apostles answered, "We must obey God rather than any human authority. The God of our ancestors raised up Jesus, whom you had killed by hanging him on a tree. God exalted him at his right hand as Leader and Savior that he might

give repentance to Israel and forgiveness of sins.
And we are witnesses to these things, and so is the
Holy Spirit whom God has given to those who
obey him."

When they heard this, they were enraged and wanted
to kill them. But a Pharisee in the council named Ga-
maliel, a teacher of the law, respected by all the people,
stood up and ordered the men to be put outside for a
short time. Then he said to them, "Fellow Israelites,
consider carefully what you propose to do to these men.
For some time ago Theudas rose up, claiming to be
somebody, and a number of men, about four hundred,
joined him; but he was killed, and all who followed him
were dispersed and disappeared. After him Judas the
Galilean rose up at the time of the census and got
people to follow him; he also perished, and all who
followed him were scattered. So in the present case, I
tell you, keep away from these men and let them alone;
because if this plan or this undertaking is of human
origin, it will fail; but if it is of God, you will not be able
to overthrow them—in that case you may even be
found fighting against God!"

They were convinced by him, and when they had
called in the apostles, they had them flogged. Then
they ordered them not to speak in the name of Jesus,
and let them go. As they left the council, they rejoiced

that they were considered worthy to suffer dishonor for the sake of the name. And every day in the temple and at home they did not cease to teach and proclaim Jesus as the Messiah

Now during those days, when the disciples were increasing in number, the Hellenists complained against the Hebrews because their widows were being neglected in the daily distribution of food. And the twelve called together the whole community of the disciples and said, "It is not right that we should neglect the word of God in order to wait on tables. Therefore, friends, select from among yourselves seven men of good standing, full of the Spirit and of wisdom, whom we may appoint to this task, while we, for our part, will devote ourselves to prayer and to serving the word." What they said pleased the whole community, and they chose Stephen, a man full of faith and the Holy Spirit, together with Philip, Prochorus, Nicanor, Timon, Parmenas, and Nicolaus, a proselyte of Antioch. They had these men stand before the apostles, who prayed and laid their hands on them.

The word of God continued to spread; the number of the disciples increased greatly in Jerusalem, and a great many of the priests became obedient to the faith. (Acts 5:12–6:7 NRSV)

Upon seeing the church at its worst, one might assume the next chapter to contain an account of the church declining, retreating, or closing down. However the next verse presents the exact opposite: "Now many signs and wonders were done among the people through the apostles. . . . Yet more than ever believers were added to the Lord, great numbers of both men and women" (v. 12, 14, NRSV).

This is followed by verses 17-22, where they were persecuted by the high priests and Sanhedrin and commanded to neither preach nor teach in Jesus' name. After being flogged and released, the disciples rejoiced for being considered worthy to join in the suffering of Jesus. Again, with the church experiencing another dark period, the very next chapter begins, "Now during those days, when the disciples were increasing in number" (Acts 6:1 NRSV).

During both the time after Ananias and Sapphira were struck dead due to perpetrating a fraud and the time after intense persecution, the number of disciples increased. The church grew. The fellowship flourished.

While confronted with a crisis due to selfishness and deceit internally and while facing intensified persecution externally, the church was not crippled by it—it increased. The church of Jesus Christ is never defined or limited by its worst moments. To be sure, the church has had some terrible moments of its own making as well as moments of persecution. Beginning with Judas's betrayal and Peter's denial, to whatever contemporary scandal we choose to name, there are plenty of dark spots for which the church has needed to repent and which many use as their reason for de-churching. However, as horrible as any of those moments or the sum total of those moments may be, the number of disciples has continued to increase. One reason why is that just as no individual is defined or limited by the worst moments of life, neither is the church.

The church is not built upon the foundation of people. It is built upon the foundation of Jesus Christ. It rests upon the revelation of Jesus being the Christ, the Son of the Living God. It is solidified and sustained by him alone. With that is the promise that he spoke to Peter, declaring that "the gates of Hades will not overcome it" (Matthew 16:18). The very powers cannot contain or constrain the church. No action from within or from without can prevent the church from achieving its mission. Neither perpetration nor persecution have the power.

STRUCTURED FOR GROWTH

The church grew. Growth presents its own set of challenges. One challenge is that of disruption. The introduction of anything constitutes a disruption which necessitates a negotiation of terms and an integration of the new into the old, forming a new and expanded whole. However, this new and expanded whole is not simply a matter of a larger shirt size. It involves a level of complexity which brings into question matters of structure, procedure, processes, and personnel.

The increase in the number of the disciples presented a challenge to the existing structure of the church. It surfaced in a murmuring between Grecian and Hebrew women concerning the daily distribution of food. Some Grecian women were not reached with food. Immediately, they portrayed the apostles as showing favoritism. This threatened to disrupt the positive momentum of the church.

Wisely, the apostles engage in a process of discernment concerning the issue. They quickly see that what the widows inferred to be a matter of personality was really a matter of an outdated structure. The current structure that they had was insufficient for the growth that they were experiencing. Their words in response indicate this:

> And the twelve called together the whole community of the disciples and said, "It is not right that we should neglect the word of God in order to wait on tables.
>
> Therefore, friends, select from among yourselves seven men of good standing, full of the Spirit and of wisdom, whom we may appoint to this task, while we, for our part, will devote ourselves to prayer and to serving the word." (Acts 6:2-4 NRSV)

It is with this that we see something else about the church and its becoming. The church is constantly faced with conflict that results from its growth and which challenges its current structures and processes. The apostles' resolution of the conflict is worth noting. They first assert the legitimacy of the Grecian widows' concern. People were not being served. They then clarify the problem being structural not personal. The current structure and process was that of the apostles receiving what was brought and also distributing to everyone. This was done on top of their giving themselves to prayer, teaching, and preaching. While that may have been appropriate for 120 people, it was unrealistic for a congregation that now was over three thousand. Remember that three thousand were added in one day alone. Having clarified the problem, they assert what is priority for them; the ministry of the Word and prayer. Consequently, they present a new structure to be added—the appointment of seven whom we call deacons.

The people gladly receive the apostles' proposal. The reception by the people is no small measure. The change in the structure would place a layer of people between them and the apostles. There would not be the same immediacy and accessibility that they had. However, they recognized that the need was worth the adjustment. The structure of the church is only as relevant as the needs that the structure meets. The emergence of new needs constantly brings existing structures and processes into question. This was profoundly seen in the wake of Covid-19. The stay-in-place order immediately challenged the existing structures and processes of every church. Those who had resisted the usage of technology-enhanced delivery of content found themselves needing to quickly adjust if they were to continue to engage congregants. The post-pandemic era presents an equally challenging time of discernment and adjustment.

Consequently, seven men are presented to the apostles for appointment. The apostles lay hands on them and pray for them. This laying on of hands is the conferral of authority for the work assigned to them. It is delegated to the seven for the work that is theirs to accomplish. The authority for anyone operating within the structure of a church is delegated for a proscribed purpose and is subject to accountability. The apostles are specific in their language: they say, "Whom we may appoint to this task" (Acts 6:3 NRSV). The seven were appointed by the apostles for the specific task of the tables. Their accountability would be to the apostles, just as the apostles' accountability was to Christ and to each other.

Biblically speaking, all who serve within the church do so within the context of delegated authority and accountability of some form.

The results of the revised structure were the number of disciples in Jerusalem increasing greatly and a great number of priests becoming obedient to the faith. The church's reach and influence were expanded and extended.

The church lived beyond its worst and grew. It has done so in every generation. May it be so in this one.

EPILOGUE

If you're reading this, you've either finished the journey or you wanted to see what the end would be before beginning or continuing to read. My aim has been for us to see the original members of what we know as the church, as people whom the Lord developed in purpose and in power. They did not fully understand what the Lord intended for them to become when they began. They discovered it over time. They did not always rise to the occasion as they would have liked or as God intended. But they discovered God's sovereign purpose to be greater than their worst mistakes.

In no way is this an exhaustive look at their development. In fact it only covers the first six chapters of the book of Acts. However, it is my hope that you've read enough, felt enough, discovered enough to have a greater appreciation of that to which God calls each person who accepts his Son as Lord and Savior. In so doing, you will help the church become what God intends in the world.

QUESTIONS FOR REFLECTION AND DISCUSSION

1—IF YOU GET JESUS, YOU GET THE CHURCH

1. Why do you gather with the church? Do you see your involvement as a commitment to God's people?

2. What usually fills your conversations? When does Jesus come up in dialogue and do you ever sense God's presence during those talks?

3. Have you thought of the church as a place to receive your "assignment"? What is God teaching you to do next when you meet together as his body?

2—SECOND CHANCES

1. In what ways do you think God has already made his will known to you? What are you still waiting to understand? How can you walk in obedience in the midst of the tension of existing between points of revelation?

2. What does it mean to you, practically speaking, to *remain* or *abide* in Jesus? What does that look like?

3. Are there any ways right now where you feel like you are "spinning your wheels"? Ways that you are expending energy but not seeing results? What might

be a way to approach the same task / person in greater obedience to Jesus?

4. Why do you think simple obedience is so hard for us when we often long for great vision and impact? What can we do to keep ourselves faithful with "the little things"?

5. Is a love for Jesus at the center of your life or do other things compete with Jesus for your time, attention, energy, or commitment? What are those things?

3—CALLED TO MISSION

1. Have you ever considered how Jesus' authority relates to where you should live? What kind of car you drive? Where you go to eat? We are to strive to make disciples in everything we do. How might you alter your lifestyle to better make relationships with and reach those around you and thus better obey Jesus' command?

2. What sorts of authorities (people, ideologies, cultural forces) do you think compete with Jesus in the United States today? Which ones sometimes tug at your heart?

3. How can you be more intentional about making disciples, whether through evangelism or through helping Christians grow?

4. Do you tend to think of Jesus as a command-giver? Why or why not? How does thinking of Jesus as a command-giver challenge and shape your faith?

5. Do you feel incorporated into the church body? How has this helped your faith? How might you be more incorporated or help to incorporate others?

6. Discipline is difficult for everyone (if it were easy, it wouldn't take discipline). What strategies or habits have you developed to help you live a life of disciplined obedience?

7. What is the significance to you, personally, of Jesus' statement that he will "be with you always?"

4—PEOPLE OF PURPOSE

1. Think back to the time before your walk with God. What made you an unlikely candidate for God's grace? Who is there in your life now that you think of as an unlikely candidate for God's grace? Pray for them now.

2. Given what you heard about how God assigns us to unusual places, given your history, where do you think God might be assigning you?

3. What most scares you about absolute obedience to God in your life today? (For example, the reactions of other people? The loss of something precious to you? The difficulty you perceive?) What promises are there in God's Word that might help push you forward in the face of those fears?

5—A DIVINE ASSIGNMENT

1. As you try to walk in obedience to Jesus, do you feel the Spirit's help or do you only feel yourself getting exhausted? How can you experience more of the Spirit's help in your walk?

2. What grade would God give you on your evangelistic assignment? Could it be that the world questions the truth of our witness because it sees so little death in us to verify our claims? What does God want you to die to? Have a discussion about how you are doing in evangelizing and how you want to get better.

3. Samaria was a place of racial conflict for the disciples, where they were to preach a gospel of reconciliation. How might God be calling you to work toward reconciliation in a Samaria?

4. God calls the apostles to take the gospel to the ends of the earth and the Bible teaches that Christ's kingdom is global. How are you engaged in the worldwide progress of the gospel? Are you praying for it? Giving toward it? Going yourself? What prevents you from further engagement?

5. How does having an expectation of a future reward change your obedience now? Do you think enough about that future reward?

6—EMPOWERED TO PROCLAIM

1. Would you say that your daily life is sustained by prayer? What can you do to make prayer a more integral part of your daily life?

2. Oftentimes we take it for granted that God always keeps his word. But how might your life today be different if you couldn't trust God to keep his word? Does this make the doctrine of God's faithfulness more precious to you?

3. Can you think of a time when the Holy Spirit led you to do the right thing even when you weren't sure what the right thing was? What was that story?

4. Reverend Dr. Martin Luther King Jr. was a great example of someone who took prophetic action based on expanded perceptions and enlarged perspectives. What areas of our country and our world today seem to be in need of this sort of prophetic action?

5. Does everything that the church does really point to Jesus? Can't the church do good in the world without pointing to Jesus? Talk about how the church should do good in the world and how that may or may not point to Jesus. (Do we have to talk about Jesus every time we do something good? Is it okay to do good things if we never talk about Jesus?)

7—A COMMUNITY OF COMMITMENTS

1. When you think about living the Christian life, how much do you think is up to you, personally, and how much do you think is up to the church? We tend to focus a lot more on our personal effort than on what we do together as a church. How might you give more weight to the church in your Christian life?

2. Psalm 1 speaks of "thinking about God's word day and night." Do you do this? What generally occupies your thoughts during the day? Are there things that you give your attention to, a little bit at a time, all throughout the day?

3. What are some of the ways that we, as a church, show our commitment to God's word together?

4. What is genuine fellowship? (As opposed to just "hanging out" or spending time together?) How would you know if you had genuine fellowship with someone?

5. What is the significance of our taking the Lord's Supper? What should we think about while we eat and drink the bread and juice?

6. What are some of the ways that we, as a church, show our commitment to prayer? To joy?

8—TRANSFORMED BY JESUS

1. Do you know how God has gifted you? Are you confident in your use of that gifting within the church?

How might others help you leverage that gift more for God's kingdom?

2. Does your life demonstrate to others the impact that following Jesus can have? Why or why not? How might your life better demonstrate the power of Jesus?

3. What is the difference between accommodating someone's life and wanting to make it better versus total transformation? How might you help others who don't know Christ understand that God wants transformation and not just a small improvement?

4. Someone once said, "The world thinks we have an intrinsic solution for an extrinsic problem, when really we have an intrinsic problem and only an extrinsic solution." What does this mean? How does it help you communicate the gospel?

5. What are some areas that you see where the church in North America has potentially verbally reached beyond what it practically offers to do, where our words don't match our actions? What could we do to demonstrate practical love in these areas? What are we doing with our hands?

6. Is your church a place where someone can feel comfortable worshiping freely and authentically? Why or why not? What do we do that hinders free expression in worship and how could we encourage more authentic worship?

9—OFFERING A WORD FROM GOD

1. Do you think that people in America today take notice of and wonder at the church? Why or why not?

2. Why should people wonder at the nature of the church? What is unusual or wondrous about what happens in the church?

3. What are the biggest changes that you saw in your life after you came to know Jesus? How could you talk about that change with others who don't know Jesus?

4. What are some of the ways that the church should really stand apart from the culture in our current time and place? Another way of asking the same question: How can God be more obvious in our churches today?

5. Given the unity that the church has around Jesus, how should community, relationships, and family look different inside the church than outside?

6. Take some time to name some things that we can praise God for, either in our experience or from what we know of him through the Bible.

10—EVIDENT BOLDNESS

1. Who is your audience? Who is paying attention to you? (Think through where you live, work, and play. And do you have a presence online?)

2. Do you think people see a difference in your life such that they may be curious about you? Why or why not? What sort of things might make a Christian stand out in this day and age?

3. Do we always plainly see the working of God in our lives? What sort of things might God be teaching us when his activity is not evident to us? What can we say to others who are in such times?

4. What is the invitation that we, as Christians, are to give to others? (Tell your neighbor in 30 seconds or less.) Why do we often hesitate to give this invitation? How might we overcome that hesitation?

11—LIVING IN THE TENSION

1. Do you find your allegiance to Jesus creates discomfort in your interactions with others? Did you expect that when you first became a Christian?

2. How do you usually navigate situations where you're tempted to diminish the importance of your faith? What could help you more boldly confess Christ?

3. Which proofs of change in your life affirm the integrity of the gospel for you? What about evidence in the lives of people you know or have read about?

4. Describe what it might look like to face times of tension empowered by the love of God.

12—HOW GOD'S PEOPLE PRAY

1. Has prayer been your first response to struggles in the past?

2. How does knowing *who* God is change the way you pray? Do you tend to address him with a particular title or identifier? If so, why do you think you resonate with that aspect of his character?

3. Pray through Psalm 118 together. Did you notice your confidence in God's faithfulness increase?

4. What does it mean to advance the name of Jesus? Is elevating the reputation of God a significant part of your prayer life? Why or why not?

13—TOGETHER IN EVERYTHING

1. Do you tend to lean on other believers when you encounter pain and hardship? Reflect on a time when you have sought support from people in your faith community.

2. In John 13:35, Jesus says, "By this everyone will know that you are my disciples, if you have love for one another." How does relational cohesion strengthen the witness of the church?

3. When have you seen the church reflect Jesus' sacrificial example by laying down influence, resources, or time?

4. What do you have at your disposal that you already offer to God and his people? How did you realize that need existed in the church and come to respond to it?

14—THE CHURCH AT ITS WORST

1. As you engage in the study life of the church, have you experienced any notable satanic influences in your life. How did you respond?

2. Since your engagement and involvement in the church, can you identify the roadblocks that challenge you in giving glory to God?

3. Why do you think *appearing* to be Christlike is a viable option for persons living out their Christian life? Why is it so appealing?

4. How have you helped someone you know who is critical about the church to understand that the church is not about us, but about God?

15—GROWING INTO THE FUTURE

1. How do you respond to the concerns of your brothers and sisters in Christ? Do you see these as opportunities for development and betterment?

2. Which structures in your congregation need adjustments for true growth to happen?

3. The apostles emphasized prayer and the Word as foundational even when reimagining the shape of their community. In what ways can your church remain steadfast in priorities during transitions?

4. What hopes do you hold for the future of the church?

NOTES

5—A DIVINE ASSIGNMENT

[1]"Lift Him Up," Johnson Oatman, 1903.

[2]"Christian Persecution," Open Doors, accessed June 3, 2022, https://www.opendoorsusa.org/christian-persecution.

6—EMPOWERED TO PROCLAIM

[1]Matthew Henry, "Commentary on the Whole Bible," vol. 6, *Acts*, chap 2, verses 14-36, "Peter's Sermon at Jerusalem," Wikisource public domain, accessed June 3, 2022, https://en.wikisource.org/wiki/?curid=3735575.

9—OFFERING A WORD FROM GOD

[1]Horatius Bonar, "I Heard the Voice of Jesus Say," public domain.

11—LIVING IN THE TENSION

[1]Pew Research Center, "Harassment of Religious Groups Continues to Be Reported in More than 90% of Countries," November 10, 2020, https://www.pewresearch.org/religion/2020/11/10/harassment-of-religious-groups-continues-to-be-reported-in-more-than-90-of-countries.

[2]"Christian Persecution," Open Doors, accessed June 3, 2020, https://www.opendoorsusa.org/christian-persecution.

13—TOGETHER IN EVERYTHING

[1]Dietrich Bonhoeffer, *Life Together*, trans. John W. Doberstein (San Francisco: HarperSanFrancisco, 1954).

14—THE CHURCH AT ITS WORST

[1]Pat Riley, *The Winner Within* (New York: Berkley Books, 1993), 52.

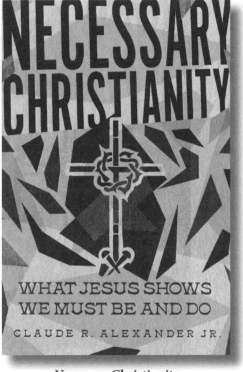

Necessary Christianity
978-1-5140-0570-5